Thomas Lovell Beddoes

Twayne's English Authors Series

Herbert Sussman, Editor

Northeastern University

TEAS 402

THOMAS LOVELL BEDDOES
From a photograph of Nathan C. Branwhite's portrait (1824)
in the possession of Pembroke College, Oxford, and used by
permission of the Master, Fellows, and Schollars.

Thomas Lovell Beddoes

By James R. Thompson

Ohio University

Twayne Publishers • Boston

For My Mother,
Elizabeth Mary Thompson

Thomas Lovell Beddoes

James R. Thompson

Copyright © 1985 by G. K. Hall & Company
All Rights Reserved
Published by Twayne Publishers
A Division of G. K. Hall & Company
70 Lincoln Street
Boston, Massachusetts 02111

Book Production by Lyda E. Kuth
Book Design by Barbara Anderson

Printed on permanent/durable acid-free
paper and bound in the United States of
America.

Library of Congress Cataloging in Publication Data

Thompson, James R.
  Thomas Lovell Beddoes.

  (Twayne's English authors series; TEAS 402)
  Bibliography: p. 132
  Includes index.
    1. Beddoes, Thomas Lovell, 1803–1849—Criticism and
interpretation.   I. Title.   II. Series.
PR4098.T48   1985   821'.7   84-15850
ISBN 0-8057-6892-0 (alk. paper)

Contents

About the Author

James R. Thompson is a professor of English Literature at Ohio University, Athens, Ohio. He received the B.A. and M.A. degrees from Bowling Green State University and the Ph.D. degree from the University of Cincinnati, where he was a Howard Taft Fellow.

Professor Thompson has written and lectured on Byron, Wordsworth, and nineteenth-century poetry and lectured in Europe on the modern American novel. He has previously contributed *Leigh Hunt* to Twayne's English Authors Series. At present he is coauthoring a study of the novelist John Irving and popular fiction.

Preface

The nineteenth-century English poet Thomas Lovell Beddoes was "a man of genius," Ian Jack has said, "who wrote nothing that is commonly remembered."[1] Yet it was not always so. In the year of Shelley's death (1822), Beddoes, still an Oxford undergraduate, published his second work and first play, *The Brides' Tragedy.* Flawed though it is, the work was favorably reviewed by important journals; and if critics recognized its weaknesses, most were excited by a freshness and an intensity lacking in other contemporary dramatists. As a result, Beddoes acquired a name associated with promise, and literary friends to encourage and promote him. For a variety of reasons he slipped into oblivion shortly thereafter. It was not until 1850, one year after his early death, that his major work—*Death's Jest Book, or The Fool's Tragedy*—was published. Except for a brief period in the 1870s and 1880s when it was fashionable among the literati to have read and appreciated him, Beddoes has remained only a shadowy figure in that eccentric category referred to as late Romanticism.

Since he willingly embraced the obscurity that engulfed him before he was even fairly launched, one might well ask why we should want to drag him back to the light now, like one of his own reluctant ghosts. The answer is simple; one finds in Beddoes's poetry a great deal of intrinsic and extrinsic interest to be explored: there are important poems to be examined and his position in nineteenth-century poetry to be determined. *Death's Jest Book* is an extraordinary production—a massive play or a poem or anthology of poetry—and simply ought to be better known. Not only does it contain some unique poetry; it also marks, like perhaps no other work, the dark side of the Romantic decline, with its obvious similarity to modern versions of despair.

"It seems as if adequate recognition has not yet been granted the author of the unhappy *Jest-Book,*" H. W. Donner lamented decades ago at the close of his admirable study of Thomas Lovell

Beddoes.[2] Unfortunately, Donner's important work did not lead to that recognition; in the years following his edition of Beddoes's works and his ambitious biographical and critical study (both published in 1935), bibliographies list only an occasional article or notice devoted to late English Romanticism's perhaps most unusual poet. However, in the last two decades several doctoral dissertations have appeared, and, more significantly, Northrop Frye has lent his impressive authority by devoting a major section of his *A Study of English Romanticism* (1968) to Beddoes's major work. Nor has recent interest been entirely literary. Eleanor Wilner in *Gathering the Winds: Visionary and Radical Transformation of Self and Society* (1975) examines Beddoes in some detail and insists on the significance of his work for our understanding of the nineteenth century and hence the modern mind. If general approval and interest remain elusive, there are at least encouraging signs that Thomas Lovell Beddoes's reputation is finally emerging. Reviewing in 1825 a play by a dramatist whom he felt to be insufficiently appreciated, Beddoes said, in words most applicable to himself: "His art is unfashionable; his productions have been not only cast aside but the distended reputations of many of his contemporaries who are much his inferiors, lie upon them like mountains, nevertheless poetry will out."[3]

For a great many early-twentieth-century critics and historians Beddoes was either an overlooked lyric genius or an important example of the Jacobean Revival in English drama. Without denying these qualities in Beddoes's work we can now see how his intrinsic and extrinsic significance can be reassessed and integrated. That Beddoes had an extraordinary lyric gift will not be denied by any reader who spends even a few hours with his collected works; however, that talent was exerted in the service of a remarkably modern if idiosyncratic vision, and it is the impressive poetic realization of that vision that not only makes his lyric poetry significant but also renders his Jacobean borrowings imaginatively important. He is not, in any sense meaningful to our age, "the last Elizabethan," as Lytton Strachey so persuasively argued at the outset of this century;[4] nor is he simply the lonely singer in the dark wood.

The present study, in emulation of the two earlier full-length studies but in a smaller compass, attempts to achieve a comprehensive understanding of Beddoes's poetry as well as his cultural significance. However, as the dates of R. H. Snow's *Thomas Lovell Beddoes: Eccentric and Poet* (1928) and H. W. Donner's *Thomas Lovell Beddoes: The Making of a Poet* (1935) suggest, the present point-of-view will diverge from past assessments; written well over forty years ago, both of these still useful examinations reflect earlier attitudes toward scholarship, criticism and, more importantly, toward Romanticism. Just as we are less interested in source study for itself than we were forty years ago, so we have long since begun to consolidate our new insights into Romanticism-as-modernism.

Because for Beddoes, as for the major Romantics, the grounds of truth are subjective, and because of Beddoes's obscurity, it will be necessary initially to discuss his life and character. The study's main approach will be, however, critical-analytical; neither biography nor literary history will be exploited for its own sake. Consequently, after an introductory chapter on Beddoes the man, we will turn to a series of chronologically ordered chapters intended to describe and explicate the work of this most unusual artist.

James R. Thompson

Ohio University

Acknowledgments

I am grateful to the Oxford University Press for permission to quote from *The Works of Thomas Lovell Beddoes,* edited by H. W. Donner, and to Routledge and Kegan Paul Ltd. for permission to quote from *The Plays and Poems of Thomas Lovell Beddoes,* also edited by Professor Donner. I wish to thank the Master, Fellows and Scholars of Pembroke College, Oxford, for permission to reproduce their photograph of Nathan C. Branwhite's portrait of Beddoes painted in 1824. Finally, it is a pleasure to acknowledge the essential editorial guidance of Professor Herbert Sussman, and the constant support and always useful criticism of my wife, Janice.

Chronology

where mother is ill. Mrs. Beddoes dies in Florence before Beddoes arrives. Meets Landor in Italy. Writes "Torrismond" and "The Second Brother." Shelley's *Posthumous Poems* published with Beddoes's help.

1825   Receives B.A. from Oxford in May. Writes "Pygmalion" and verse-letter to Procter. Leaves England for Germany in June and matriculates at Göttingen University on July 27. Begins *Death's Jest Book*. At Göttingen until September 1829.

1826   Writes second verse-letter to Procter.

1828   Visits England and takes M.A. at Oxford; visits London and Amsterdam. Returns from second visit to London. Completes *Death's Jest Book*.

1829   Sends *Death's Jest Book* to England, where its extensive revision is urged by Procter and Bourne. Deeply depressed; attempts suicide. After a severe drinking bout is sent down from Göttingen. Matriculates at Würzburg in October. At Würzburg until 1833.

1830   Writes "Dream-Pedlary." *Poems, Chiefly Lyrical* (Tennyson).

1831   Joins *Germania Burschenschaft*. Takes M.D. in September. Publishes political articles in *Volksblatt*.

1832   Ordered deported from Würzburg. Imprisoned for debt in order to escape dismissal. Leaves in July. Goethe dies.

1833   Living in Zurich. Matriculates at the university in April. Publishes "Lines Written in The Prometheus Unbound" in *Athenaeum*. Sister Mary Eliza dies. In Zurich until 1840.

1835   Visits Brussels, Canterbury, and London. Recommended for chair of anatomy but rejected by Zurich board of education.

1838   Rents theater and acts role of Hotspur in *Henry IV*.

1839   Residency problems; rematriculates at the university.

1840   Leaves Zurich in April and lectures on drama in London in June. Travels to Berlin and matriculates at the university in November. *Sordello* (Browning).

1842 At Berlin; visits London.

1843 At Baden and Zurich. Wordsworth made Poet Laureate.

1844 At Zurich, Baden, Basel, Strasbourg, Mannheim, Frankfort, Giessen, Berlin. Publishes anti-Jesuit poems in the *Republikaner*. Writes "Lines Written in Switzerland." Revises part of *Death's Jest Book*.

1845 At Frankfort, Zurich, Baden.

1846 At Frankfort. Visits London, Shifnal, and Cheney Longville for the last time.

1847 Leaves England in June. At Frankfort. Suffers long illness after cutting himself during a dissection.

1848 Leaves Frankfort for Basel. Opens artery in left leg on July 18, the day after his arrival, and is taken to hospital.

1849 Dies in Basel Hospital on January 26. Buried in hospital cemetery January 29. Maria Edgeworth and Edgar Allan Poe die. *The Strayed Reveller* (Arnold).

1850 *Death's Jest Book* published by Kelsall. Wordsworth dies. *The Prelude* (Wordsworth). *In Memoriam A.H.H.* (Tennyson).

1851 *Poems Posthumous and Collected of Thomas Lovell Beddoes. With a Memoir* published by Kelsall.

Chapter One

The Man

The story of Thomas Lovell Beddoes is important first as the life of a valuable poet.[1] But beyond providing a background for readers of *Death's Jest Book,* Beddoes's life is interesting as a modern instance—the story of a psychic alien, a man so essentially modern that his wandering existence becomes an appropriate metaphor for the contemporary human condition. There are qualitative similarities between Beddoes's life and both real and fictional embodiments of modern angst—for instance Edgar Allan Poe and Dostoyevsky's Underground Man. The problems of reason and imagination, faith and despair, which define that sensibility, remain central issues of our time.

Clifton and Edgeworth Town

Beddoes's childhood, indeed his whole life, is marked by a diverse heritage. Clifton, where he was born in June 1803, was the location of his father's surgery and laboratory. Thomas Beddoes, who had long since come to be known as the "celebrated Dr. Beddoes," was a physician and scientist of considerable fame in his own day and a man well equipped to open doors for his son later, even on the Continent. The senior Beddoes was a man of his time: universal in his interests, devoted to the principles of the Age of Reason, eccentric in his personal habits. He belonged to that extraordinary provincial group known as the Lichfield Circle, which included Thomas Day, author of *Sandford and Merton;* Erasmus Darwin, the naturalist and grandfather of Charles Darwin; Anna Seward, the poet; inventor Richard Lovell Edgeworth and his novelist daughter Maria. Generally speaking these people were, as John Heath-Stubbs calls them, "left-wing intellectuals":[2] disciples of Rousseau, supporters of the French Revolution (for which Dr. Beddoes lost his very popular chair of chemistry at Oxford), proponents of progressive education, students of the entire range of human affairs.

Dr. Beddoes was also the friend of literary men of the stature of Southey, Wordsworth, and Coleridge, the latter of whom sincerely admired the scientist and had long hoped to write his biography. A source of some amusement to us now as the founder of the Pneumatical Institute (where he experimented with laughing gas and persuaded Coleridge to try it), Dr. Beddoes in his own day marked a new stage in the liberation of experimental science. His early and devoted disciple was the future Sir Humphry Davy, the eminent chemist.

While Dr. Beddoes was a deeply reticent man, despite moments of flashing humor, his wife, Anna Maria Edgeworth, was charming, open, warm, vivacious. She possessed a generous share of the imaginative sensibility of her inventor father and novelist sister. According to Humphry Davy, who was for a time a member of the Beddoes household, Anna "possessed a fancy almost poetical . . . and, under favourable circumstances she would have been, even in talent, a rival of Maria," the novelist.[3] If Dr. Beddoes bequeathed to his son an extreme rationalism and a dedication to science as an avenue to ultimate truth, Anna Beddoes gave him the imaginative spark that, surviving the scientific career, produced the plays and poems. Though the poet would argue that science and poetry were allied and complementary pursuits, his life actually illustrates a classic example of the Romantic reason-imagination conflict. The two poles of his childhood existence—Edgeworth Town in Ireland, where he was taken to visit his literary relatives, and his father's surgery in Clifton—aptly symbolize a schizophrenia from which he would never escape.[4]

Thomas Lovell Beddoes was not yet six years old when his father died and he was removed from the influence of the Clifton laboratory. He had very probably witnessed there his father's dissection of various animals—unlike his friend Wordsworth, Dr. Beddoes did "murder to dissect"—an activity intended to teach his children not only about animal life but also about the sexual processes. Beddoes was a precocious child; no doubt such scenes would have had an unusual impact on him. But the legacy of the dissecting table need not have been literal, nor would it necessarily have been entirely positive. Beddoes's lifetime obsession with the dead or dying body, with the mystery of spirit and matter, may have resulted from experiences too complex to be absorbed by one possessed of such a vivid yet immature imagination. His father was, moreover, a dynamic, imposing man, one capable of successfully exploring a whole range of experience; his death would, in the context of his own role as healer, strike Beddoes with awful force.

Charterhouse and Oxford

Beddoes's childhood was punctuated by visits to the Edgeworths in Ireland, where Maria read to the children and provided theatricals for their entertainment, and trips to Cheney Longville, the prosperous estate of Dr. Beddoes's second cousin, Thomas Beddoes, Jr. In 1814 Mrs. Beddoes moved her family (there were by the time of Dr. Beddoes's death two brothers and two sisters) to Bath, where the boys entered Bath Grammar School; in 1817 Beddoes entered Charterhouse School. His life as schoolboy at Charterhouse and undergraduate at Oxford shows us an already distinctive personality: willful, perverse, independent, and precocious. At public school he mastered English drama, wrote two long Gothic tales, invented a slang language long perpetuated by Charterhouse students, and emerged a lively, eccentric figure—one respected if not necessarily loved. One has the impression of something already distant about him, as though amidst all the activity and intense relationships of public-school life he was yet alone, if not lonely.

In 1820 Beddoes matriculated at Pembroke, Oxford (his father's old college), and continued against school authority his guerrilla warfare begun at Charterhouse. Despite normal pranks and dissipations, however, it was during this period that Beddoes's literary talents emerged and rapidly developed; almost the only work to be released during his lifetime was published while he remained at Oxford: *The Improvisatore* (1821) and *The Brides' Tragedy,* the following year. The former work was very immature and highly derivative; later, when he had come to recognize and reject its obvious badness, he recalled unsold volumes and carefully cut out and removed from the binding any copy he discovered in a friend's library. But the publication of *The Brides' Tragedy* made him more than a student celebrity;

reviews were largely very positive, citing his clear mastery of
blank verse and the play's originality and emotional power.

By 1824 Beddoes was, at twenty-one years, a twice-published
author; he had sat for his portrait and in May of that year had
begun the examinations for the B.A. degree. However, before
he could complete the examinations he was called to Italy, where
his mother, who had been living in the South for her health,
had fallen ill. Mrs. Beddoes died before her son arrived at Florence, and he was able only to escort his sisters back to England.
Her death is a significant turning point in Beddoes's life; with
his second parent's death he felt the cold winds of time blow
directly on himself, changing him from a literary connoisseur
of death to a man deeply concerned with its profound significance.

Göttingen versus Grub St.

Beddoes's literary and Bohemian life at Oxford had yet allowed him a conventional academic career; he had received
the B.A. in 1825 and returned to the university to take an
M.A. in 1828. At this time Beddoes's life underwent what only
appears to be an unexpected turn. It would seem that following
Oxford the obvious course for Beddoes, as a talented young
man of modest but independent means, would have been a
move to London, there to test his literary possibilities, and a
career in law had once been mentioned. But despite two publications and several encouraging, even laudatory, reviews before
he reached his majority, Beddoes elected science, not art, as a
career. In this choice we see the still-powerful influence of Dr.
Beddoes, dead before the poet reached his sixth birthday. By
the time Beddoes had determined to study medicine in Germany
(where, though he did not originally intend to, he was to spend
most of the remaining phase of his life) the long self-exile had
begun.

His attitude toward poetry, moreover, was already changing.
Arriving in Hamburg in July 1825, before moving on to the
University of Göttingen, where he was soon to matriculate,
he described himself as being with "meerschaum at his side,
full of grave & abundantly prosaic" intentions (605). At first
he was sure that "the studies then of the dramatist & physician

are closely, almost inseparably, allied," but he wondered whether one man could contain both professions (609). It was not long before he was insisting on a complete shift in loyalty: "to tell you truly I begin to prefer Anatomy &c. to poetry, I mean to my own, & practically; besides I never c^d have been the real thing as a writer: there *shall* be no more accurate physiologist & dissector" (618). We see here his sense of creative inferiority, an attitude that largely accounts for his history of textual revision and reluctance to publish. He even claims to "have left off reading Parnassian foolery" (619). At this point the anatomy of the body was, one guesses, so much more definite than the anatomy of the soul. By 1827 he declared his absolute "preference of Apollo's pill box to his lyre" and his choice of "Göttingen instead of Grub Street" (the home of hack writers) for his abode (636).

Yet despite repeated declarations like these, Beddoes continued to work on *Death's Jest Book,* commenced in 1825; he also wrote lyrics and read and extensively commented on German literature, especially Schiller, Goethe, and Tieck. At first things seemed to go very well. Brilliant as well as capable of hard work, he was soon strongly impressing his professors and outperforming "the labourious Sauerkrauts" (618). Göttingen's famed professor of medicine J. F. Blumenbach would later declare that Beddoes was the best pupil he had instructed in fifty years of teaching.

But if anatomy and other medical studies led to a very considerable competence they had not, as he had hoped, led to a quantum leap in knowledge. Nor did the 1828 completion of *Death's Jest Book,* sent to his friends Bryan Walter Procter and J. H. G. Bourne in 1829, bring compensatory rewards; back in England they insisted on various serious revisions that he felt incapable of performing. With the progress of both scientific and poetic vocations blunted, his letters began to display a quietly increasing melancholy. Already "the truth was restless in him, / And shook his visionary fabrics down" (103). In 1829 he probably attempted suicide; that he suffered severe depression is clear. Drunkenness and disorderly behavior, now the sign of inner turmoil and not undergraduate high spirits, caused reluctant university officials to order him to be sent down from Göttingen. He had arrived there in good spirits, dedicated to unlocking the deepest secrets of human life. He left, he said, "already so thoroughly penetrated with the conviction of the absurdity and unsatisfactory nature of human life" that he could only "search with avidity for every shadow of a proof or possibility of an after-existence, both in the material and immaterial nature of man" (630–31).

Then he rallied. Leaving Göttingen he moved to Würzburg, where he matriculated just two months after having been summoned before the university court and, subsequently, relegated. He was to remain in Würzburg until 1833, taking the M.D. in 1831, though he would never practice professionally. Here he greatly added to his store of political and scientific friends, many of whom would share his life later in Zurich. Most important, in 1831 he was made a member of the student political organization *Germania Burschenschaft,* a rare, probably unique distinction for a foreigner. This organization worked for the unification of Germany and the elimination of its many princes under a constitutional monarchy. The membership reflects Beddoes's fellow students' keen admiration for his abilities and vigorous political integrity. It also suggests the continuing influence of his father and Beddoes's heightened political awareness. For Beddoes and many of his generation, both English and German, there was no division between cosmic and Continental politics. But it may have been that political involvement also offered Beddoes meaningful activity in a world where art and science had already largely failed him.

Subsequently he shared with his liberal and radical allies many speakers' platforms and political journals. His medical studies continued also, as did his investigation into German philosophy. Yet despite the fact that he felt acutely the impact of linguistic isolation—he claimed to be losing his native tongue—whenever possible he would become "a truant from the old bones / And winds of flesh" in order to pursue the "satiric pathos," as he put it, of *Death's Jest Book* (613, 614). The effect of his literary isolation and his skeptical attitude, however, was an increasingly odd and introverted poetry. He predicted that his play would "come with its strangeness" as "an electric shock among the small critics" from whom he expected "cunning abuse" (617).

From 1833 to 1840 Beddoes lived largely in Zurich, caught up in liberal politics, continuing medical studies and social life.

He had been forced to leave Würzburg because of his political
agitation, and the Bavarian police records provide us with a
description of him at this time: "Height 5′ 7″, hair light brown,
forehead high, eyebrows fair, eyes dark, nose fairly long and
pointed, mouth big, chin rather prominent, face oval, complex-
ion pale, build slight, neglected clothing, light grey coat, white
breeches, and either in English fashion or as German hero of
Hambach one boot black, the other red, and on one of them
a gold or gilt spur, speaks bad German, fair moustache, bad
teeth."[5] These years were, relatively speaking, perhaps the most
stable and moderately happy of his later life; he had many
friendly companions if no real friends. In 1835 he visited Brussels and London with the famed Dr. J. L. Schönlein, his revered
professor from Würzburg; in the same year Beddoes was recommended by the faculty at Zurich University for a chair of anatomy but was denied the post by a board of education hostile
to his politics. The forced resignation of Zurich's radical govern-
ment in 1839 marked the end of this period in Beddoes's life
and in the spring of 1840 he began a final nine years round
of wandering. He stayed or visited principally in Berlin, Baden,
Zurich, Frankfurt, and Basel. In 1842 and again, for the last
time, in 1846–47, he returned to England. During this time
he seemed visibly to grow much older, a strange pilgrim search-
ing for a shrine he had no expectation of finding.

The Final Act

Meanwhile Beddoes continued to pursue in his scientific studies and macabre poetry the politics that really haunted him,
the politics of mortality. Self-exiled from England (now "Cant-
land"), to which he returned only infrequently, Beddoes had
permanently assumed the role of a Faustian searcher after ultimate knowledge. Dipping his scalpel repeatedly into the mystery
of nameless dead Germans he reminds one vividly of his friend
Mary Shelley's unfortunate Dr. Frankenstein. Declaring death
a "dotard," Beddoes still hoped to "unmask all his secrets; make
him play / Momus o'er wine by torchlight. . . . / To conquer
him and kill. . . ." So he rationalized, since "contempt grows
quick from familiarity. / I owe this wisdom to Anatomy" (614–
15). In this tormented quest his imagination struggled with his

reason for the prerogative; the final victory of his scientific heritage—of Clifton over Edgeworth Town—could impede but not utterly subdue his poetry. However, the failure of either approach to yield up truth left him spiritually paralyzed and brought him, finally, to suicide, at Basel, Switzerland. There on a July morning in 1848 he used his scalpel for the last time, opening an artery in his leg. Saved at Basel Hospital from death (though doctors eventually found it necessary to remove his leg as a result of infection caused by his attempts to reopen the wound), Beddoes took poison and died on January 26, 1849. He was forty-six years old.

Beddoes's acceptance in 1829 of his friends' timid advice to revise further the completed *Death's Jest Book* produced a barrier to his imagination that it never fully overcame. As a Romantic writer, of course, he more or less accepted the concept of art as self-therapy. But each time he felt the urge to compose, the presence of the yet-unpublished *Death's Jest Book* would channel his creative energy into revision and enlargement rather than into fruitful new areas. Had he published in 1829 there is an excellent chance that the sheer release afforded—whatever his public success—would have made possible a larger, less idiosyncratic artistic development. Instead, Beddoes turned away from potential readers and critics and burrowed ever more deeply into his own narrow obsessions.

Moreover, there was the problem of his nearly complete creative isolation. "The best things come, as a general thing, from talents that are members of a group," Henry James argued in his analysis of the impact of the lonely Salem years on Nathaniel Hawthorne; "every man works best when he has companions working in the same line."[6] Although Beddoes's life was filled with academic and political friends, he was excluded both from any sustaining emotional relationship and any vital literary contact with his English contemporaries. His European sojourn, never intended to last long, had become permanent exile and in no way nourished his poetic career—rather, it made extensive creative dialogue impossible.

His early promise forgotten long before he died, Beddoes was lost to his generation and subsequent generations of readers. In England only his old friend Thomas Forbes Kelsall and a few others remained faithful to his potential. In 1850 Wordsworth's long since written *Prelude* was published, reminding the high Victorians of the Romantic dawn. In the same year Kelsall brought out *Death's Jest Book;* but it was much too late. Beddoes's unpublished works, manuscripts and biographical materials, loyally protected by Kelsall against even Beddoes himself, were bequeathed to Browning, who, immensely impressed by the dead poet's talent, planned on making him the subject of his first lecture, should he be appointed to the chair of poetry at Oxford. But Browning, with his own work to pursue, delegated the editing of Beddoes's materials to Edmund Gosse. Gosse made a start on the papers in the "Browning Box," as it came to be known, and then it disappeared. Dykes Campbell, another tenacious admirer, had fortunately made copies of the most important items earlier, but readers would have to wait until 1928 and 1935 for complete editions to be published. It is not surprising, therefore, that Beddoes remained a coterie poet in the nineteenth century.

However, before Beddoes sought out Keats's "easeful death" he had transformed *Death's Jest Book* into a vehicle for his compelling fascination with final concerns. This poem, or collection of poems—bizarre, grotesque, often hauntingly lovely and certainly mordantly witty—demonstrates that despite the frequently noted influence of the Jacobean playwrights, his true peers may actually be Poe and Baudelaire. The voice, however, is distinctly his own; in all of English Romantic poetry there is nothing quite like this work. Unfortunately for Beddoes, his perspective made it impossible for him to realize this unique accomplishment; nor had his father's science, to which he had subordinated his imaginative life, produced the key to the secret of mortality for which he so vainly searched. Neither imagination nor reason could identify the Bone of Luz; his bifurcated quest for a means to transcend the world's remorseless harm was a failure.

In a note scribbled just before drinking poison, Beddoes asserted that for him "Life was too great a bore on one peg & that a bad one," and noted wistfully that he "ought to have been among other things a good poet" (683). He had always underrated his own talent, preferring to remain in obscurity rather than swell the ranks of tasteless rhymers. Perhaps he ought to have been a great poet; he had clearly been a very good one.

Contemporaries often assumed that Beddoes's self-destruction was the result of madness, and some modern critics imply that homosexual tendencies may have caused sufficient self-loathing to produce such an act. That Beddoes possessed at least latent homosexual characteristics seems likely; it is still unclear whether he lived with or at least supported a handsome young German baker. But there is no evidence that guilt of that variety produced suicide, and the accusation of madness appears to be as much a cultural indictment as a psychological analysis. He was an eccentric to be sure; among the stories of his odd behavior is the one concerning his attempt to set Drury Lane on fire with a lighted five-pound note during his last visit to England. But setting fire to the theater was, on one level, the drunken sanity of a dramatic antiestablishmentarian, and, on another, the good sense of the fool, the jester, the honest participant in human disorder. In any case, "neurosis may be the occasion but literature is the consequence," as Philip Rahv says about Kafka.[7] Actually, in Beddoes's case, so-called madness was simply a radical view of the human condition, and suicide the carefully selected alternative to a painful existence. In a strange sense it may even have been an act of faith.

Chapter Two

The Improvisatore
and Other Poems:
Borrowed Clothes

Beddoes's early prose and verse tales—including *The Improvisatore*—and his incidental lyrics are largely the product of reading rather than life. Except for some of the lyrics, all are immature and few possess much intrinsic merit. In this chapter we will examine Beddoes's early compositions and first published poetry; our concern will be with those chief influences on his work evident in varying degrees throughout his life but here largely borrowed, not possessed, and we will see the first signs of preoccupation with certain characteristic subjects and themes. Beddoes was steeped in Gothic literature; this background, along with Romantic poetry and his growing appreciation of Renaissance drama, affects especially the atmosphere of his work. Among the Romantics, Beddoes admired chiefly Shelley. It is therefore not surprising that Shelleyan idealism, fragmented and naive, should tinge even the more grotesque of these works. But with Shelley as with the Gothic and Jacobean, the effect is largely in detail, not in substance.

There are, however, some signs—obvious only in retrospect—of his future originality. These appear mainly in an occasional peculiarity and richness of imagery and, of course, in subject matter. Although *The Improvisatore* is intended as narrative, the poem comes really alive only in its descriptions, a characteristic of the young Keats's work as well. And death abounds—albeit in the trappings of popular culture; though there is little of its later, intensely personal significance, his preoccupation here may not be entirely derivative.

"Scaroni, Or the Mysterious Cave:
A Romantic Fiction"

In 1818, when the fifteen-year-old Beddoes, by then a student at Charterhouse, composed his "Scaroni," the Gothic novel, though still very popular, was nearing the end of its long tenure. Charles Maturin's *Melmoth the Wanderer* was still two years away; however, Horace Walpole's prototypical *Castle of Otranto* had appeared in 1764 and the genre, along with the Gothic drama it influenced, was largely a product of the eighteenth century. Even in 1797 Coleridge—several of whose best-known works are marked by obviously Gothic influences—could argue in his review of the soon-to-be famous *Ambrosio, or the Monk* that "the horrible and the preternatural have usually seized on the popular taste, at the rise and decline of literature."[1]

One of the early modern associations with the word romantic had been with Gothic fiction. Even if one rejects Montague Summers's assertion that Gothicism is the essence of Romanticism,[2] that the genre in some general but important way reflects the breakup of Enlightenment literary taste and the shift toward the Romantic sensibility cannot be doubted. As an early stage of an evolution (later to become a revolution) the Gothic, with other "non-Augustan" works, reflects the new imaginative and emotional subjectivity; it is clearly a part of the emerging literature of process.[3] Recognition of the Gothic element in Beddoes's later work is crucial to an understanding of his peculiarly Romantic nature, especially since Gothicism itself is influenced by and merges with the revival of Jacobean drama, another of Beddoes's strong enthusiasms.

However, Beddoes's attempt at the form in "Scaroni," despite its significant subtitle, is simply another of the many early and late imitations inspired by the genre. The work is cliché-ridden in language ("Phillippo's blood froze in his veins" [501]), in detail ("the ground emitted flashes of blood-red lightning accompanied by immense claps of thunder and a shower of hot blood!!!" [506]), and in narrative. The hero of this congested and directionless little story is a young Italian nobleman, the Marquis de Scaroni. Traveling with two servants through a winter forest, he is captured by a giant savage dressed in wolfskin and smeared with blood. One servant is overlooked by the giant and his retainers, but Scaroni and the second servant are locked in a dungeon from which they eventually escape twice, the second time successfully with the help of the first servant. Before leaving the prison they kill a nest of poisoners and rescue a drugged woman. Upon returning to his father's castle, young Scaroni discovers that the woman he has freed is his own mother, who has been unaccountably "lost for a long time" (518). Arbitrarily inserted into the main narrative are two unrelated stories of a similar fantastic nature. Mercifully, the entire piece takes up only eighteen pages in the collected works; once the reader has finished he desires no more. Beddoes wisely chose to leave the piece unpublished.

The range of Beddoes's borrowing here is difficult to measure, but clearly extensive;[4] literally nothing may be his own. However, the gallows humor of Scaroni's servant Gobbletti does point ahead to the macabre (although more bitter) mixture of horror and grim comedy that is the hallmark of *Death's Jest Book,* and there are several other such theoretical parallels. Of these, one may be significant. In the first of two inserted stories the realms of life and death temporarily merge and one of the characters—a living woman called to death by her dead sister—speaks "about death as of some great good" (508), an argument repeatedly implied or directly stated in Beddoes's later work. To make very much of these elements would be overly ingenious; utterly to ignore them would be to deny a possible, if tenuous, continuity.

The Early Poetry

Beddoes's earliest poetry is only a little more encouraging than his prose tale "Scaroni." Written perhaps while still at Charterhouse, all but one were rejected from the group of "other poems" referred to in the subtitle of *The Improvisatore,* published one year after Beddoes entered Oxford in 1820. Except for an isolated line or image, they cannot detain us with their intrinsic merit, but they help mark the growth of his talent.

Of these early attempts three poems, all unfinished, show us Beddoes groping for a subject and a theme; they indicate as well some major influences and interests. The two versions of "The New-Born Star," though differing in details, tell us

that "the world is born today" (10) and go on to describe a
lovely natural world with neither people nor yet their ghosts,
which emerges "leaf after leaf, and glory under glory" (5).
Even without man or sin Beddoes cannot avoid a forward glance;
the "death-intending wrinkles" on the sea's brow suggest that
he is "the murderous Judas of the world" (11).

Both versions of "The New-Born Star" (but especially the
one subtitled "A Fragment") remind us of the young Shelley:

> And from the breaking air
> A waking music did unbind
> Its curls of pale invisible hair
> And in veins and rivers wind
> Round the crest and bosom fair
> Of the foundling world. . . .
>   (5)

The celebration of the world's newness is muted; both versions
are wistful in their sense of the beauty and innocence of a world
where "death had not a grave" (5). And Beddoes, in what is
probably the latter of the two attempts, introduces lines that
suggest George Leopold Cuvier's theory of evolution as a series
of created and destroyed worlds:

> Over many a star
> And the interstellar vale,
> Through which some aged patient globe
> (Whose gaunt side no summers robe),
> Like a prisoner through his grate,
> Shivering in despair doth wait
> For sunbeams broken, old, and pale.
>   (10)

Byron, who himself had applied Cuvier's theory in his drama
Cain, is either imitated or parodied in the most interesting of
Beddoes's juvenilia: "Alfarabi, The World-Maker." Donner,
who sees Beddoes imitating Byron—"the careless easygoing
iambs, the mocking tone, and the sarcastic parentheses, make
parts of it almost a pastiche"—thinks that the young poet originally set out to write a serious philosophical poem, "perhaps
even to rival *Cain*," and then succumbed to comic temptation.[5]

It is true that the 170 lines suggest greater ambition than do other early poems, yet with the exception of the ending, it is mainly in the first thirty-four lines that the Beppo-like quality exists, and they may actually satirize Byron. For example:

> but where are we?
> I see: 'twas in those days that Alfarabi lived;
> A man renowned in the newspapers:
> He wrote in two reviews; raw pork at night
> He ate, and opium, kept a bear at college:
> A most extraordinary man was he.
>
> (6)

Yet immediately following this passage come several well-written lines the seriousness of which will echo throughout all his later work, and these lines suggest not only Byron's Cain, but also Manfred:

> But he was one not satisfied with man,
> As man has made himself: he thought this life
> Was something deeper than a jest, and sought
> Into its roots: himself was his best science.
>
> (6–7)

The narrative, confused with strange descriptions (it was to be, as the subtitle suggests, "A rhapsodical fragment"), relates the space and possibly the time travel taken by a sleeping man's soul. For the young Romantic it was not "Logic" or "her crabbed sister, Metaphysics" that provided "the secret and the spell / Of life," but rather "his own mind, / The lamp that never fails us" with which "he read the mystery" (7). Like Byron's Cain, Alfarabi enters that Romantic world of space travel and it carries him to the "very boundary and brim / Of the whole universe" (8), and in so doing again reminds us of Shelley. Then the poet, lapsing into his earlier satiric style, has his visionary, arrived now at the "End of all, the Universe's Death" (9) force the dead to create another world. And here the poem ends in mid-sentence, Beddoes having reached the point beyond which his youthful imagination (was it his wit?) could not carry him. Later Beddoes, commenting on the strangeness in seeing the "fossilized faces of one's forgotten literary creatures years after the vein of feeling in wh they were formed, has remained closed and unexplored" would ask "what the devil is 'Alfarabi'?" (662).

Yet, for all its immaturity, uncertainty of tone, and intellectual naiveté, the poem remains interesting to the student of Beddoes's work and development. First, there are some fine lines (e.g., ll. 16–22), some modest wit, and something, too, of his later blend of grim humor and deadly earnestness in his exploration of "the universe's suburbs" (8). But perhaps of greater importance are the clues one finds to his later attitudes and themes. The contrast between reason and imagination (ll. 47–53) not only reflects the orthodox Romantic doctrine but also foreshadows his own more specific lifelong conflict between science and poetry, an internal conflict both philosophical and psychological. To the end of his life he would struggle with the world's "unheeded hieroglyphics," desperately hoping to find the "secret and the spell" (7). Unable to succeed, he would elect his single choice, perform the one experiment still open to him—the taking of his own anguished life.

The Improvisatore: The Gothic Poet

The epigraph to this little volume, with its all too descriptive title and motto borrowed from Webster, tells most readers all they care to know about the work: "I have sung / With an unskillful, but a willing voice." Both claims are true, though the second fails to redeem the first. The epigraph, along with the subtitle—"Three Fyttes"—indicates that literary rather than experiential inspiration is largely responsible for the work. It was probably inevitable that, considering the manner and matter of these tales, a reviewer would employ the obvious pun: "fits, indeed! hysterical decidedly," suggesting that these tales were excessive even for the age.[6] Beddoes himself, only five years later, would write Kelsall that he envied him the "pleasure of dissecting & laughing at such a grotesque fish as the Improvisatore" (618).

The work is essentially derivative; there are Gothic shades and Shelleyan ghosts in these loosely connected narratives and, of course, a heavy Jacobean atmosphere. These tales lack the sardonic wit and intensity of his later poetry, or even many sure signs of special talent. And yet we cannot afford to simply ignore this little volume of "Three Fyttes With Other Poems," imitative as it largely is. In the first place, it is one of only two volumes published by Beddoes in his lifetime. Moreover, despite the typical Gothic horror and conventional sentimentality, we can discover a kind of vague apprehension of the material of his major plays, as well as the themes that would haunt him throughout his short life. It is therefore chiefly interesting for marks of influence, as a starting place, and, more important, for the first faint traces of a distinctive Romantic personality struggling to free itself from the imprisonment of borrowed clothes.

The three fyttes are held together by a storytelling frame not only loose and conventional but inconsistent as well. The induction to the first story assumes a comfortable winter evening on a knight's estate, an occasion—after sufficient food and drink—calling for a tale "of love, or war" from a "wandering minstrel boy" (16). When the young troubadour concludes his performance he leaves the hall to ramble in what now has become a summer night's "fringy green" (27); here for no particular reason he meets a young woman named Agnes who requests a "tale of fairy lore" (28). Upon completion of the second tale, his audience having "tripped to court a night's repose" (39), the boy meets "an old and tottering crone" (40) who bribes him with rare wine to produce the third and final fytte. Beyond the clear situational and even verbal echoes of "The Eve of St. Agnes," the reader is struck by the total inappropriateness of these inductions to the tales themselves, three stories of increasing horror.

In the first, "Albert and Emily," two betrothed young lovers manage to fall asleep in a forested valley on the eve of their marriage. They are awakened by a storm of unusual violence and clearly supernatural overtones. While taking shelter under an ancient oak, Albert—but unaccountably not Emily—is struck dead by lightning. The next day her maids find her wandering "with an idiot stare" after which she "gamboled back" to the shattered oak, only to burst "into a roar / Of hideous laughter" at the "shapeless, black, and incoherent mass" that had been her lover (24). Perhaps even a decidedly unimpressed modern reader may be a little shocked by Emily's state of mind when "that loathsome lump she hastened to embrace" (25). If he is moved, however, her sudden flight deeper into the woods "with a discordant whoop" breaks the mood; the whoop is indeed discordant. Emily spends an increasingly passive and witless summer until, in the autumn, she is found dead on Albert's obligatory grave. Commemorative plants—"a thornless rose and lily"—obligingly and of course quite spontaneously mark their mutual grave (27).

The second fytte tells how Rodolph, a young shepherd of the pastoral rather than agricultural variety, is lured on by a haunting music and gigantic fiery hand to a lovely cave where a beautiful woman awaits him. The instant he swears, upon command, to be hers only, the vision dissolves and he is in a charnel house, Circe's island, Acrasia's "bower of bliss," or La Belle Dame's hillside turned into a chamber of death, with "many a steaming splash / Of melting flesh" showered on him in this "body-jammed vault" (37). The sexton eventually finds him (like Emily) insane, playing with bones and decomposing flesh. Crawling out of the tomb he too spends an indefinite period wandering witless in the woods before being found "dead and cold" (39).

The third fytte, not to be outdone, opens on a silent battlefield so littered with the dead and dying that it appears "as if the flesh had been snowed on the hills / And dribbled away in blood-clammy rills" (41). An ancient and generous hermit rescues from his dead mother's breast a smiling babe "who laughed, and held his blood-tinged fingers up; / His lip was moist, as though he'd made a cup / Out of some foaming wound" (42). Taken in and gently raised by the hermit, who names him Leopold, the child grows up cold and sullen, refusing to accept religion or even the old man's love. Like Browning's Caliban, Leopold spends his days sprawled in a low, fetid cave entwined in snakes and tickled by "hideous crawlers" (46). Eventually he becomes a sort of passive Faust; offered by evil forces the power to tour the universe if he will kill his benefactor, Leopold accepts, and after only a slight hesitation, stabs the old man to death.

Rewarded for his deed by "heels winged with flame," Leopold becomes a Cain-like wanderer "among the elements" (48) and returns to earth after centuries, only to fall in love with a young woman seen through a cottage window. His very look, however, kills her and, after a return to his "fatal cave" (and another supernatural storm), he leaves forever.

Beddoes was right when he repudiated these tales; they possess, beyond a few lovely lines, little of intrinsic merit. He can describe the stars as "gold-scaled fishes struggling / In flimsy purse of fisher's rings" (15), foreshadow destruction with a sinister sunset likened to a "red wound, that blushes in the west" (29), or (using a favorite image) compare a shower of sparks to "a swarm of . . . fiery bees" (32). He can also find the first stirrings of love "like the busy whisper of morn in its youth" (31). This last line is found in "The Madrigal" of the second fytte, a poem Donner admires beyond anything else in the volume: "this is the boy at his best and most characteristic. The pleasant conceits, and the playful elaboration, the accumulation of images, all this will return in his mature poetry."[7] So they will, but these moments are very rare in *The Improvisatore*.

Moreover, while the poem may point toward his mature and original poetry, it also suggests his debts. The weakness for excessive description supplied as compensation for a lack of action, for example, reminds us of Keats's early problems. More obvious still, the rapid piling up of similes (for example in lines 51–58 and 63–66, where each line starts with "as") is clearly reminiscent of Shelley's lyrics, especially such poems as "The Skylark."

Beddoes's diction is generally weak throughout the tales; neoclassical clichés mingle with Huntian archness. Though reflecting a convention his readers would understand, the plots seem absurd now and, as noted earlier, totally inconsistent with their frames.[8] More important, the sensationalism has no thematic basis; it is simply theatrical exploitation. It is perhaps significant that the horror—which increases with each fytte—is more nearly Gothic than Jacobean. His taste is already changing, as *The Bride's Tragedy* will demonstrate, but here, as Snow observes, he is too inexperienced and young "to realize the distinction between the shudder of physical horror and the shudder of the soul."[9]

Death, so excessive as to neutralize any serious impact on the reader, floods the pages. Yet we have seen that as early as the unpublished "Scaroni," Beddoes makes a character speak

of "death as of some great good" (508), and in each of the
three fyttes we can detect not only his early obsession but something of his future attitudes. Emily embraces "that loathsome
lump" (25), which has been her lover; she laments not so much
his death as the fact that he has left her behind. Rodolph in
the second fytte sits "among the tombs" and speaks of the dead
"with voice familiar" (38). Finally, a significant passage in the
third fytte raises the tale's only important question:

> What is this life, that spins so strange on
> That, ere we grasp and feel it, it is gone?
> Is it a vision? Are we sleeping now
> In the sweet sunshine of another world?
> Is all that seems but a sleep-conjured ghost,
> And are our blind-fold senses closely curled,
> Our powerful minds pent up in this frail brow,
> But by our truant fancy? Are we a groping host
> Of sleepers, gazing in this twilight gleam,
> Unconscious dupes of some thought-peopled dream?
> But I will think no more, lest haply I,
> If I erred on in thought's dim wilderness,
> And scared myself with shadows, ne'er should die,
> But my astounded soul might petrify,
> And freeze into time-scoffing stoniness.
>
> (45)

Donner regards Leopold, whose anguished lines these are, as
a "real demon inspired by his own wickedness."[10] His behavior
is obviously evil; yet it is less clear that his behavior stems from
so pure and simple a condition. The question he raises, after
all, is Beddoes's own, a question Donner admits the poet will
raise again and again in future works. It may be too far-fetched
to see in these lines the poet's death wish, yet what the last
few lines suggest may well make us wonder. Snow is correct
in warning us against totally ignoring here "that fatal impinge-
ment of the other world upon this."[11]

The Quatorzains

The remaining poems in Beddoes's first slender volume consist of thirteen "Quatorzains" preceeded by "The Comet" and

followed by "To a Bunch of Grapes." On July 6, 1819, the *Morning Post* had printed Beddoes's "The Comet," his first published poem, thirty-four lines in clumsy couplets not very originally titled, considering the celestial phenomenon then so much in evidence. This work is notable only for its complacent patriotism, which asserts that, despite this "demon's" wholesale destruction, "Britain, unhurt, shall endure to the last" (51). Two years later, when Beddoes gathered up odds and ends to flesh out his first published volume, he was obviously desperate enough to include this completely immature work as one of the "other poems" in the title. The volume's concluding poem, "To a Bunch of Grapes," has been described as "the glory" of the individual lyrics, "an exquisite arabesque of playful imagination, where the central idea, like the variation on a theme in music, strays away only to return, and returns repentant only to stray again."[12] This seems excessive praise. It is unquestionably a finer attempt than "The Comet," both in Beddoes's control of versification and in his treatment of the subject. But its subject is an enameled nature, something closer to that of Leigh Hunt or the early Keats than to that of Wordsworth; its saccharine juices and odors rapidly cloy. Beddoes may well have chosen to conclude the volume with this work in order that the reader might leave the book on a warmly sensuous, cheerful note—if so it indicates an interesting self-awareness. At any rate it clearly alters the tone of the double quatorzain that immediately precedes it, a poem to which we must return in a moment.

The term "quatorzain," meaning a fourteen-line poem not in the typical sonnet patterns, is curious; why did the young poet go out of his way to suggest but clearly reject the sonnet? While using a concluding couplet he employs two sestets in place of the normal English and Italian rhyme schemes, which consist of three quatrains and a couplet in the first instance and an octave and sestet in the second. He obviously wishes to try something different—we are reminded of Keats's transformation of both sonnet forms into his personal ode—and elsewhere Beddoes speaks of the sonnet as an "uncouth animal with fourteen legs / And jingling feet" (171). But surely he realized that the alternate rhymes he employed "jingled" as well. Moreover, the form is too restrictive for the development of any very complex idea and yet misses the lovely unity of the traditional sonnet. Curious, too, is his lack of interest in a form so highly valued by the Elizabethans he deeply admired.

For the most part the quatorzains are mere exercises occasionally graced by a felicitous line or made pleasant by virtue of a clever conceit. They contain some unpleasant lines reminiscent of the half-dozen or so frequently cited to damn Shelley, for example, the one ending "tears, the pure blood drops of the wounded soul" (53). Diction is often weak, including many Augustan clichés such as "pinions" and such popular romantic expressions as "Cobweb-limbed ephemerae" (52).

Some of the more conventional poems, as in the early work of Keats, are intended to celebrate the role of the poet or the nature of poetry itself. In "Thoughts," for example, his youthful enthusiasm is touching, though not very convincing. "Sweet are the thoughts that haunt the poet's brain" he tells us in the first line, and then offers us a Shelley-like set of poetic correspondences: "rainbow-fringed clouds," incense "from rocking censer," the mist "from out the slender cowlip's bee-scarred breast" (52). In "To Poesy" he salutes the "sweet sister of my soul" whose "kindly agony" comes with "gushing tears of sound" (56). But here he has also learned that poetry can bury its "sharp fang" in his "heart's core" (56). Born of a scientific father and soon to dedicate himself to that same perspective, Beddoes yet cannot—and never will—ignore the siren song of the muse, or avoid the pain she must cause.

But more interesting than this typical Romantic obsession with poetry is the indication that the young poet already recognizes the limits of his art; "man's puny words" and his "grovelling thoughts" (57) cannot save him from the "huge, viewless ocean into which we cast / Our passing words," words that "sink away" while only "an echo bubbles up upon the blast" (55). This use of sea imagery in several of these poems is remarkably like Byron's continual reminder of the "watery outline of eternity" in *Don Juan*.[13] For Byron "this nautical existence" represents not only the ceaseless flow of life but also its inescapable oblivion:

> Between two worlds life hovers like a star,
>   'Twixt night and morn, upon the horizon's verge.
> How little do we know that which we are!

> How less what we may be! The eternal surge
> Of time and tide rolls on, and bears afar
> 　　Our bubbles; as the old burst, new emerge,
> Lash'd from the foam of ages; while the graves
> Of empires heave but like some passing waves.[14]

In the best of the quatorzains (11) Beddoes makes Byron's image of the "watery outline of eternity" even more immediate by anticipating our inevitable drowning in the sea of time: "we all must sink / Still grasping the thin air." In "frantic pain / Grappling with Fame to buoy us" we are forced to recognize that "the sea's vast treasury" is sealed off, even to "Eternity, by whom swift Time is slain" (56–57). In these lines there is little doubt that we are in the presence of an anxiety that will inform his work until the very end. It is not surprising that in *The Brides' Tragedy,* to which we must now turn, Beddoes's anxiety results from an acute sense of the problematic nature of existence itself.

Chapter Three

The Brides' Tragedy
and Dramatic Fragments:
Jacobean Romantic

As we approach an examination of Beddoes's *The Brides' Tragedy* and other dramatic attempts, it will be useful to pause for a brief discussion of the significance of his choice of drama as a vehicle for self-expression, as well as our critical attitudes toward that choice.

"Mental Theatre"

The earliest of Beddoes's reviewers and many critics since have treated *The Brides' Tragedy* and *Death's Jest Book* as drama, either in some abstract, almost Platonic sense or as an example of a neo-Elizabethan or Romantic version of the form. Such an approach is nearly impossible to avoid, despite the quite undramatic sprawl of *Death's Jest Book* and Beddoes's own assertion that *The Brides' Tragedy* was intended "exclusively for the closet" (172). In addition to his two published plays there are the host of dramatic fragments and false starts, his generally strong admiration for playwrights (especially those of the Renaissance), and his own keen observations on the stage.[1] His description of *The Brides' Tragedy* as a work designed to "court the reader in lieu of the spectator" (172), and his insistence in the preface that the glory of contemporary English drama exists in such productions, must be contrasted with his slightly scolding comments in a letter to Kelsall: "You are, I think, disinclined to the stage: now I confess that I think this is the highest aim of the dramatist, & I should be very desirous to get on it. To look down on it is a piece of impertinence as long as one chooses to write in the form of a play, and is generally the result of a consciousness of one's own inability to produce anything striking & affecting in that way" (640). This observation was made not in the first enthusiastic moments of playwriting but in 1829, seven years after *The Brides' Tragedy* had been published and at least one year after the completion of *Death's Jest Book.*

But unlike some Romantics, he actually makes slight distinction between closet drama and the stage; Beddoes would not agree with the American poet and critic Elder Olson in supposing that "everyone would agree that a universal and absolute condition of drama is the possibility of its being *enacted.*"[2] In fact, he would have agreed with Byron, who declared the wish to make a *"regular* English drama, no matter whether for the stage or not, which is not my object,—but a *mental* theatre."[3]

Beddoes and Byron are supported in this matter by modern theorists; Kenneth Burke, for example, calls genres "strategies for living." They are "fundamental ways of thinking about, organizing, and managing the vast, confusing swirl of life."[4] Northrop Frye sees genres as mythoi that shape rather than imitate life. Drama provides a specific "radical of presentation," the rhetorical structure of which in part predetermines significance, since in literature, as in language, form helps determine meaning. Hence if "a Romantic poet gives his poem a dramatic form, he may not expect or even want any stage representation; he may think entirely in terms of print and readers; he may even believe, like many Romantics, that the stage drama is an impure form because of the limitations it puts on individual expression. Yet the poem is still being referred back to some kind of theatre, however much of a castle in the air."[5]

Our realization of the significance of generic choice—even in the use of closet drama—is therefore an essential justification for considering Beddoes's work as drama, however unsuccessfully it may fulfill such obligations of that form as plot and characterization. Yet the problem of generic choice is for Beddoes, as for other Romantics, too complicated for the theory of genre alone to resolve. In the first place, the nature of generic determination does not, in itself, explain why the form was chosen. Equally important, the theory accounts for a general set of circumstances surrounding the work's significance; it must be made to take into account the relationship between the specific sensibility and the form.

We may start with the second issue as a means of returning to the first. Drama is, or traditionally was, a most objective form. The innumerable and unsuccessful attempts to get to the man behind Shakespeare's plays epitomize simultaneously the aesthetic distance found in drama and the common assumption that playwright and audience share values. Yet Romantic poets both wished to and were forced to explore the personal nature of truth, and the meditative lyric—that most private of public forms—was for them its chief expression. Terry Otten, in words especially relevant to Beddoes, puts one resulting difficulty perfectly: "Adopting Elizabethan dramaturgy to express modern subjective matter was too much like grafting an alien myth onto a new vision. The modern concern with the individual and the internal 'dialogue of the mind with itself' worked at odds with a communal drama directed to a homogeneous body of believers."[6]

Yet Beddoes, Shelley, and other Romantics (the significant exception was Byron) did attempt to embody in Elizabethan dramaturgy a truth the grounds of which were clearly subjective.

Much modern poetry, indeed much poetry generally, has been classified by Robert Langbaum[7] as "the poetry of experience"— that is, a poetry that does not assert propositional truth but rather explores it, does not prescribe reality but describes it. This is a poetry of process; it reflects the poet's mind in search of the significance of its own experience. Why then, in an age when such poetry emerged from the chaos of fragmented values and discredited mythologies, did Beddoes—and Byron, for that matter—elect the drama at all? The answer would appear to be found in the question; in many subtle personal ways as well as in broadly cultural ones, traditional drama had once reflected the very cosmic and cultural stability that was missing. In other words, the genre could suggest the very *shape* of value—a form historically associated with the testing of social norms or public myths, and with a celebration of their endurance. In this sense both tragedy and comedy had worked together to dramatize and endorse those values. Hence the more that modern culture disintegrated and writers like Beddoes imaginatively experienced that disintegration, the more nostalgia they felt for a form that seemed to receive its license from a permanently organized universe, a universe that reflected its organization in its cultural artifacts.

It is unlikely that Beddoes was aware of the ironical nature of his own commitment to the form; though he understood his failure in conventional terms he does not seem consciously to have recognized the retrospective longing in his choice. But this schizophrenia of personal experience and public form leads to the paradox of Beddoes's drama. The subjective material is forced into objective form, and whatever his self-awareness, the tension produced helps to account for the unusual energy and character of *Death's Jest Book*. Beddoes's contemporary George Darley, a poet and critic, was fully aware of the problem: "Subjective composition is however the natural tendency of our refined age, and on this postulate founds itself an argument I fear convincing against the probable regeneration of Acting Drama. Can we restrain that tendency? or *should* we, if we could? Though fatal to the drama, it may be vital to something else as desirable."[8] The poetry of experience was vital to Beddoes's self-expression; and though not fatal to the drama, it demands a special awareness on the part of the reader.

If Beddoes failed to understand the deeper implications of his choice, his judgment of the contemporary theater was nonetheless acute. Like other Romantics unable to escape the enormous pull of Shakespeare—"he was an incarnation of nature . . . he was an universe" (581)—Beddoes was all the same aware of the dangers of emulation. Only three years after *The Brides' Tragedy* was published and in the year he began *Death's Jest Book* (1825), Beddoes made a statement rare for its combination of good sense and overpowering self-irony:

Say what you will—I am convinced the man who is to awaken the drama must be a bold trampling fellow—no creeper into worm-holes— no reviser even—however good. These reanimations are vampire-cold. Such ghosts as Marloe, Webster &c are better dramatists, better poets, I dare say, than any contemporary of ours—but they are ghosts— the worm is in their pages—& we want to see something that our great-grandsires did not know. With the greatest reverence for all the antiquities of the drama, I still think that we had better beget than revive—attempt to give the literature of this age an idiosyncrasy & spirit of its own; & only raise a ghost to gaze on, not to live with— just now the drama is a haunted ruin. (595)

Byron, too, recognized the error in "following the old dramatists." For him, however, the danger results from the Elizabethan ignorance of classical regularity; he chastised Shelley for using "our old dramatists *as models.*" He goes so far as to deny "that the English have hitherto had a drama at all."[9] Beddoes, for some curious reason, thought that *The Cenci* had been inspired by the Greeks and lamented that Shelley had not chosen Shakespeare "as his model" (578). It goes without saying that numerous critics and historians of the drama have seized upon Beddoes's "reanimation" argument as an example of Romantic myopia, which, of course, it is.[10] Yet Beddoes was compelled to the drama because he believed deeply that it "ought to be the most distinguished department of our poetic literature" (624), and drawn equally to the late Elizabethans because they provided an ambience perfectly suited to his own sense of a world become sick, evil, and decayed. It is obvious that for Beddoes the Elizabethans and Jacobeans were the drama.

Beddoes's relationship to the drama is important, then, more in its broad configuration than in its specific nature. A study of his plays on purely technical grounds will take us little beyond the long-since established indictment of Romantic failure in that genre. On the other hand, the assumption that the choice of closet drama was merely superficial ignores the deeper meaning in such a decision, as well as its significance for interpretation. Failures of plot construction and character development do not remove the importance to be found in the identification of genre with myth and vision; it is in this larger sense that we should view Beddoes as a playwright.

"A Very Sad Boyish Affair"

As he did almost all his other work, Beddoes eventually repudiated *The Brides' Tragedy* (637). Written when he was nineteen, the play certainly has a "boyish" quality; yet despite its excesses, the work is much more than juvenilia. The play is to Beddoes what *Endymion* was to Keats—both a necessary act of apprenticeship designed to marshal and mature his poetic talent and the first real articulation of his personal vision. There are signs here of his own characteristic grotesque; during the vicious storm in which Hesperus murders Floribel the "Night with giant strides stalks o'er the world, / Like a swart Cyclops, on its hideous front / One round, red, thunderswollen eye ablaze"

(204). And when the protagonist finds death in the bottom of his cup—"the sugar of the draught"—we catch the characteristic sound of the later Beddoes (208).

The plot, attacked by some critics for being too loose and by others for being too academic, is consciously designed with the actual stage in mind, yet unconsciously burdened with non-dramatic intentions. It was clearly planned to observe the dramatic unities, the events occurring in a severely limited period of time and an equally restricted area of action.

Act 1 opens with a private garden meeting of Hesperus, a young nobleman, and Floribel, his secretly married wife. Although theoretically it is a joyous occasion, an ominous tone of "fickleness, and woe, and mad despair" (177) creeps in with Floribel's reported dream and with the song "Poor old pilgrim Misery." Scene 2 reveals Orlando, another young nobleman, plotting to force Hesperus to marry his sister Olivia, so that he himself can marry the supposedly unwed Floribel. In order to "scare a rival and to gain a brother" (178) Orlando has had Hesperus's elderly and impoverished father arrested for debt; if Hesperus will agree to the wedding, Orlando will end this "show of cruelty" by freeing Lord Ernest and canceling his debt (178). In scene 3 Hesperus's father is discovered in prison, outwardly brave but ready to plead with Hesperus to comply. In the face of Lord Ernest's pathos Hesperus finds it impossible to explain his dilemma and agrees to the second marriage.

In Act 2, after an interval in scene 1 where we see Orlando with his page boy, the action shifts to the cottage of Mordred and Lenora, Floribel's high-born but impoverished parents. Floribel, ignorant of his problem, teases Hesperus. Faced with his lovely and much-loved bride, Hesperus mutters, "why let the old man die" (188), referring to Lord Ernest's prediction of his own destruction, should Hesperus fail to save him by marriage to Olivia. He leaves but returns to find Floribel giving Orlando's page an innocent kiss, having actually first torn up Orlando's letter of proposal. Hesperus, convinced she is unfaithful, repudiates her. Scene 3 finds him back in Orlando's palace, where he woos and wins Olivia, promising her true love only in the grave, however. Left alone by the troubled but acquiescent Olivia, Hesperus implies a threat to murder Floribel. Scenes

4 and 5, also located in the palace, show us first a tormented Hesperus waking from a terrible dream and fighting the desire to murder Floribel and then the troubled realization of Hesperus's deranged behavior by Lord Ernest, Orlando, Olivia, and Claudio. The concluding scene in this act occurs at a suicide's grave; first Orlando and Claudio speculate on a "self-slaughtered" parricide and then, after their departure, Hesperus soliloquizes at this "shrine of blood' (198,199), pledging himself to evil.

The five scenes in act 3 take place in Orlando's palace, Mordred and Lenora's cottage, and a dark wood. While Hesperus sits in a deep trance in the palace, Floribel broods at home on his strange behavior and gives voice to her premonition. During a terrible storm in a wood, Hesperus meets Floribel and stabs her to death. Hunters see him burying something and, as he leaves to seek his "second bride," they linger on to discover his "hoard." In the palace we witness Olivia's sentimental farewell to her maids. This pleasant interlude is immediately followed by a grim scene in Mordred's cottage. Just when Lenora has informed Mordred that his last wish—for Floribel to marry well—has been fulfilled, the hunters enter with Floribel's body. The already feeble Mordred dies of grief and shock.

Act 4 opens with a deeply agitated Hesperus—now far gone in evil—vowing to kill a servant whom he suspects of knowing his secret. He has fixed on Olivia as his only salvation. In scene 2 Floribel's murder is reported to the duke, who, since Hesperus has left his easily recognized dagger in her grave, orders his immediate arrest. We next observe a banquet hall in Orlando's palace, where, before the mystery of Hesperus's strange behavior can be cleared up, officers come to arrest him. The act's final scene takes place in the street before the duke's palace; we first see guards, Floribel's body, and Lenora. When this group leaves, Hesperus, his father, and Orlando arrive. The act concludes with Hesperus hoping that Olivia might not also die, since "there are enough accusers in the tomb" (225).

Like acts 1 and 4, act 5 is short. The remaining four scenes in the play take place at Mordred's cottage (where Lenora, now also deranged, believes Floribel to be only asleep), at the ducal prison, at Orlando's palace, and at the place of Hesperus's intended execution. In prison we find Hesperus condemned to die for the murder, deeply confused about death and guilt. Lenora enters and begins to curse a Hesperus now beset by "Remorse and Conscience" (227). But because Floribel has loved him and he her, Lenora extends to him her disturbed sympathy. After Olivia prepares for death in scene 3, the play concludes in a scene set at the place of execution. Hesperus, now calm and contrite, is reconciled with his father. Just before he is executed, Lenora saves him from the ax with the perfume of poisoned flowers. He dies in an agonized vision of murder coming at him with "fiery fangs."

"Dark Thoughts"

One death from grief and another inevitable; two suicides; one murder—what are we to make of this body-strewn play written by a young man not yet twenty? Both Beddoes's peers and reviewers, as well as his early modern critics, thought that they had the answer. He was, in the best-known statement of this argument, "the last Elizabethan." When Lytton Strachey[11] made this claim in 1907 it summarized a long-standing opinion; since then it has been frequently repeated. It is difficult to argue with several generations of critics.

Nor, up to a point, should we. Strachey, Donner, and D. W. Goode[12]—to name but three—have carefully studied and noted the parallels between Renaissance drama, especially later versions, and Beddoes's work; these critics differ mainly in their judgment of his success. Certainly a subject so thoroughly covered needs no detailed analysis here. Moreover, even the casual reader of Renaissance drama will recognize the characters, situations, and even language distinctive to that great period of English theater. Already as a schoolboy Beddoes had been immersed in the genre; like that of earlier Romantics his admiration for these playwrights was unbounded. Even his beloved Shelley, he thought, had too little followed Shakespeare "as his model" in *The Cenci;* close knowledge of Shakespeare and the Elizabethans was, he felt, essential for any dramatist (578).

But Beddoes's saturation in Elizabethan drama and the resulting evidence in his work should not cause us to substitute study of influence for study of specific plays. When Allardyce Nicoll in his history of the English stage dismisses *The Brides' Tragedy* as simply "dark thoughts culled from Jacobean drama,"[13] he misses the point completely. Beddoes's claim that "reanimations are vampire-cold" (595) is completely serious; the irony should not blind us to the two essential characteristics of Beddoes's work that develop in this period. First, he is no mere imitator as in *The Improvisatore,* but rather feels a deep, imaginative affinity with these great predecessors in horror; in the Renaissance sense of the word he "possesses" these works. Second, *The Brides' Tragedy* illustrates how completely he has absorbed and modified the Romanticism of his age. The real significance of the play, despite its remarkable exploitation of Renaissance drama and its surprisingly successful blank verse, is its peculiar embodiment of late Romantic pessimism and preoccupation with death—in image, symbol, and theme.

There is, moreover, the question of source as opposed to influence. If influence accounts, at least superficially, for Beddoes's treatment of his source, the source itself is not Renaissance drama. In his preface Beddoes claims his play to be "founded upon facts" (172) and cites the ballad "Lucy" by Thomas Gillet, published in *The Midland Minstrel* (1822). This poem, and a slightly different prose version that Beddoes also employed, tell the supposedly true story, set in the early eighteenth century, of the secret marriage of a well-bred Oxford student to a college servant's daughter and his later murder of the girl when a better match presents itself.[14] As we will see, Beddoes alters the story significantly, not only by completely changing the context but, more importantly, by providing the murderer with a very different motive. Although Donner attributes these changes to a sort of Romantic reflex action, Beddoes's alterations of the source of *The Brides' Tragedy* reflect—as does his special use of generic influences—the personal, if confused, nature of his theme.

And confused the play is, despite the relentless, even mechanical, logic of Hesperus's destruction of others and himself, suggested by the plot summary given earlier. Behind the bewildering though exciting mixture of melodrama, eloquence, and sentimentality, underneath the variety of motives for the murder, lies Beddoes's own ambivalence concerning death— one from which only death could free him. But since it is the theme of the play, not its action, that concerns him, and since that theme is connected with states of mind, the usual objections to the flawed dramaturgy or to a distorted reality produced by that dramaturgy have little significance. The action, in other words, is metaphorical, not sociohistorical. The work "dramatizes," in the largest sense, Beddoes's spiritual, and hence aesthetic, predicament; the choice of drama provides an occasion for poetic eloquence and a reassuring, traditionally significant container for a radically pessimistic vision, yet resolution is not possible. In other words, the form offered Beddoes what the ballad offered Coleridge in *The Ancient Mariner,* a precious moment of closure so essential to the artist if he is to go on creating. However forced and tentative that closure was, he was never to achieve it again. For finally, the "dark thoughts" were Beddoes's own, not Jacobean, and the play looks as much toward the modern theater of the absurd as it recalls the Renaissance.

Eros and Thanatos

The Brides' Tragedy is not a fully mature piece and we must not judge Beddoes by this work alone, even though it is his only technically complete play. However, both stylistically and thematically we have come much closer here to the view of life in Beddoes's major work. Although the deaths here may appear to be of the essentially Jacobean variety, Beddoes's peculiar obsession with all of its manifestations points ahead to *Death's Jest Book* and the late lyrics. But more specifically, the love story takes a characteristically ominous turn. Hesperus kills Floribel, his secret wife and first love; he then offers the alternate bride a consummation in death: "for when our souls are born then will we wed; / Our dust shall mix and grow into one stalk" (193). The metaphor of birth is neither ironic nor simply rhetorical. "Death's darts are sometimes Love's" (490), Beddoes will later argue; Thanatos and Eros join in all his major poetry and this identification becomes a central theme in *Death's Jest Book.* It is in the exploration of this theme that modern criticism most significantly alters and improves earlier studies of the poet.

The association of love and death can of course be found elsewhere in Romantic literature. Eric Bentley, commenting upon the Romantic element in Strindberg's plays, points out that the Romantic "rediscovered *eros* and *agape* precisely by rediscovering their ambivalence. It is the ambivalence of *eros* in Goethe's *Werther* that made the book at once a great scandal and a great event. Any eighteenth-century hack might have rhapsodized about passion; it was the closeness of passion and death, of creative love and its contrary, that Goethe put his finger on."[15]

The English Romantics also touched on this theme. A classic example is John Clare's "An Invite to Eternity." Here the woman is invited by her lover to pass through "night and dark obscurity" to the ideal world beyond: "Say maiden can thy life be led / To join the living with the dead / Then trace thy footsteps on with me / We'er wed to one eternity." In Shelley the apotheosis of love leads essentially to its destruction in the transcendent but static state. For Keats the woman can be the demon lover, as "La Belle Dame Sans Merci" suggests; in a similar way love is distorted or destroyed in Coleridge's "Christabel." Even in the satiric-comic mode of Byron's *Beppo* the lovers' gondola is likened to a coffin. More surprising yet are Wordsworth's "Lucy poems," each a testament to love and death. With Poe, of course, the identification is frequently dramatized, as for example in "The Fall of the House of Usher."

In Beddoes, who like Poe is a late Romantic, the theme is more central and more overt than in other English poets. In the source of *The Brides' Tragedy,* for example, the murder is purely social in origin. In the ballad "Lucy" the student is inspired by "ambition" (709) and in the *Oxford Herald* version, after meeting an aristocratic young woman, the student again returns to Lucy but now views her "only as a bar to his ambition" (711). In the original, therefore, the story is an early version of *An American Tragedy.* But Beddoes rejects that motive, overtly at least, for three others: Hesperus must escape his first marriage in order to save his father; he is jealous of Floribel after seeing her kiss a page; and he suffers periodic madness. One of the conventional dramatic weaknesses of the play is the confusion these three motives produce. But the murder is actually symbolic; its significance is not to be found in plot. Hence Beddoes's argument in the preface that the play dramatizes the "contest of duties and desires" (173) inherent in Hesperus's situation represents his conscious intention (and certainly dramatic tradition) but not the play's real conflict—the clash between conventional human norms and the deeply felt sense that only in death can love be realized.

While avoiding the intentional fallacy we can yet recognize the determined manner in which Beddoes's vision leads him from the middle-class, domestic tragedy of his source to a frightening study of the demon lover, a study that makes itself felt far more significantly on the symbolic rather than the narrative level. And nowhere is that determination more pronounced than in the play's first scene. Its dramatic logic is clear; at once we recognize the fragility of the relationship between Floribel and Hesperus. They love each other deeply, and have married for love, despite the threat of displeasure by Hesperus's "austere and old . . . sire" (176). But there is no hint of a solution given; Hesperus lacks the will to devise their escape. And for all her love for Hesperus, Floribel cannot overcome the dismay she feels at her "sad and lonely fate / Thus to be wed to secrecy"; on her husband's face she sees only the "blank and ugly vizor of concealment" (175).

Moreover, the scene opens in growing darkness and takes place in a closed "bower of Eglantine" where "not a spark of prying light creeps in, / So closely do the sweets enfold each other" (174). This delightful privacy of love gives way to images of imprisonment, secrecy, and concealment, especially with the "tale of blood" (174) Hesperus chooses to tell Floribel. At first the story appears perfectly gratuitous, quite unnecessary to the dramatic action, and to be used simply as an excuse for Beddoes to indulge in "poesy" and Greek myth. The story tells how Zephyrus (ominously associated with the West) "once found / The baby Perfume cradled in a violet" and how after he had "bound the sweet slumberer with golden chains," he cast the "fettered wretch" into "the bosom of a rose." There the helpless child's "heart's blood stained" the flower, giving it its traditional color (175). Floribel, who in a lovely Keatsian passage has been previously associated with her gift to Hesperus, the "blue violet, like Pandora's eye, / When first it darkened with immortal life" (174), fails to see the story's meaning. But the reader—though probably not the theater audience—recognizes the tale for what it is, a rather Blakean parable of entrapment and death. Frye points out that Floribel, the "veiled Moon's . . . loveliest nymph" (174), is not a Diana as we might expect, but a Proserpine.[16]

Before the scene ends Floribel tells Hesperus of a waking dream she has had, a dream that starts in her world of passive, floral beauty and ends when one "who with wet downcast eyelids threw aside / The remmants of a broken heart" bid her be " 'ware of love, / Of fickleness, and woe, and mad despair" (177). Hesperus's response is to sing her a song, "Poor old pilgrim Misery," and to promise—in words now inescapably ominous—that they would soon meet "to part never more" (178). The scene, at first glance appearing cluttered and unsure, has established far more than a vague sense of apprehension appropriate to the play's future action; it has presented and developed the tone and imagery of the Eros-Thanatos theme so central to the entire work.

"Now for My Second Bride"

By the end of the first act any possible solution is gone. Hesperus can murmur, "wed / Olivia; there's damnation in the thought" (181) but he cannot bring himself to tell his father why marriage is impossible. Lord Ernest, whom critics fail to recognize as well drawn, is lost in self-pity; he cannot see the terrible effect his plea has on Hesperus. The latter, an essentially passive character, from this point on can only react. His deep pessimism springs from the frustration of impotence and a profound sense of the world gone wrong:

> Why are we tied unto this wheeling globe,
> Still to be racked while traitorous Hope stands by,
> And heals the wounds that they may gape again?
> Aye to this end the earth is made a ball,
> Else crawling to brink despair would plunge
> Into the infinite eternal air,
> And leave its sorrows and its sins behind.
>
> (183)

This sentiment may seem exaggerated, given his predicament and its apparent solution. But Beddoes makes Hesperus flawed, if not already spiritually defeated, from the start; other characters hint at some strangeness always recognized in him (186, 188). Moreover, the play's first scene indicates that love, the single redemptive force the work offers, can succeed only when hidden outside life. In a scene effectively juxtaposed to the grim one that precedes it, the conventional Orlando can speculate that "the universe's soul . . . is Love" (185), but for Hesperus love means death. Hence his murder of Floribel is a kind of consummation, or would have been had he joined her. Instead, coerced by his father and Orlando, he lives to woo Olivia. The lovemaking is both extraordinary and sudden. Olivia, long in love with Hesperus, ignores the suddenness and, though troubled by his strange appeal, yields.

In some of the play's strangest lines, Hesperus defines the nature of their mutual realization:

> Then thou shalt be mine own; but not till death.
> We'll let this life burn out, no matter how;
> For when our souls are born then will we wed;
> Our dust shall mix and grow into one stalk,
> Our breaths shall make one perfume in one bud,
> Our blushes meet each other in a rose,
> Our sweeter voices swell some sky-bird's throat
> With the same warbling, dwell in some soft pipe,
> Or bubble up along some sainted spring's
> Musical course, and in the mountain trees
> Slumber our deeper tones, by tempests waked:
> We will be music, spring, and all fair things
> The while our spirits make a sweeter union
> Than melody and perfume in the air.
> Wait then, if thou dost love me.
>
> (192–93)

Something in this passage reminds us of John Donne—for instance the line "our dust shall mix." But we are actually much closer to Shelley; the "sweeter union," like other hints of consummation in the play, is sexless. Hesperus celebrates the briefest passage of time, for it will bring their union closer: "Joy, my love, / We're nearer to our bridal sheets of lead / Than when your brother left us here just now" (193). However, Beddoes gives no indication as to how death can be more than an escape into stasis. Olivia, essentially more spiritually healthy than Hesperus, knows that "it is not good / Thus to spurn life," but asks, "what's to live without my Hesperus? . . . I'll be nothing rather" (194). It is Hesperus himself who, despite his conviction of death's release, asks the obvious, though unanswerable, question:

And do those cherries ripen for the worms,
Those blue enchantments beam to light the tomb?
Was that articulate harmony, (Love uses
Because he seems both Love and Innocence
When he sings to it,) that summer of sweet breath
Created but to perish and so make
The deads' home loveliest?

(194)

But Beddoes has no answer.

The entire issue remains unclear. Floribel's mother, Lenora, recognizing the "loathed blessing of a cursed existence," asks "where thinkest our spirits go?" A minor character can answer only with pretty rumor:

Madam, I know not;
Some say they hang like music in the air,
Some that they lie ingirt by cloudy curtains;
Or 'mong the stars.

(222)

In a similar way Olivia's maid, facing the impending death of her mistress, hopes to persuade herself that this "intercourse / Of disembodied minds is no conjecture, / No fiction of romance" (231). Overwrought by Floribel's murder Lenora must "search about for Comfort," and though others may call him death, "Comfort is his name" (223).

In the play's final act Olivia can sincerely repudiate man's conventional fear and horror at the thought of dying:

Death! thou silly girl,
There's no such thing; 'tis but a goblin word,
Which bad men conjure from their reeking sins
To haunt their slumbers; 'tis a life indeed.

(230)

But exactly what kind of "life"? At first it appears to be vaguely Christian, and that is the sentiment Olivia no doubt wishes to convey:

> These bodies are the vile and drossy seeds,
> Whence, placed again within their kindred earth,
> Springs Immortality, the glorious plant
> Branching above the skies. What is there here
> To shrink from?
>
> (230)

However, death immediately becomes not a door to immortality
but a welcome oblivion:

> Though your idle legends tell
> How cruelly he treats the prostrate world;
> Yet, unto me this shadowy potentate
> Comes soft and soothing as an infant's sleep,
> And kisses out my being.
>
> (230)

The "shadow potentate" who, in that marvelous clause "kisses
out my being," is Eros-Thanatos—the gods of love and death
become one. The imagery, and hence the implication, is even
clearer in Floribel's speech in the third act:

> Come so to me, sweet death, and I will wreath thee
> An amorous chaplet for thy paly brows;
> And on an odoured bank of wan white buds
> In thy fair arms
> I'll lie, and taste thy cool delicious, breath,
> And sleep, and sleep, and sleep.
>
> (202)

Again the erotic becomes the static; love-as-death is not sexual
passion, not ecstasy—only relief. At least in *The Brides' Tragedy,*
love is not, as one critic has argued, "the force that keeps death
from being the end."[17] Rather, the lover has, to use Keats's
words, to its "high requiem become a sod."

Near the play's conclusion Hesperus, demon wooer of both
women, admits that all he knows of death is "that 'twill come"
(232). Perhaps "our minds share not corporeal sleep, / But
go among the past and future," or possibly "inspire another
[life] in some waking world" only to die yet again (233). But
unlike other characters Hesperus is a murderer; beset by the

"hounds of Lucifer" he feels "Remorse and Conscience too" (227). Although his final lines exhibit some of the spirit of Byron's Manfred, who, though dying, can still repudiate external control, the ending more nearly reminds us of *Dr. Faustus.* Hesperus now associates death with punishment, although the play, only vaguely Christian, is ambiguous in this regard. Life may be our "ailment," as he earlier argues, but at least for Hesperus death is no cure. And if some cosmic law finally claims him, even a static consummation of love in death is impossible.

Eleanor Wilner, in her interesting analysis of Hesperus, extends the love-death theme considerably. Recognizing the extremely passive nature of Beddoes's women, she sees Hesperus's murder of Floribel as a perversely self-saving act; wishing to live himself he seduces others to death. "The killing of Floribel is the killing of tenderness in himself," a tenderness he "seems to equate with a passive and helpless femininity." For Wilner, death in Beddoes's world is a "purely male force."[18] Critics have long noted the passive nature of his female characters, it is true, and not only does Hesperus murder Floribel, he also brings about the deaths of her mother and, inevitably, Olivia. Yet Wilner's argument presumes a far more active Hesperus than the play offers us. He actually shares the female passivity; action is thrust upon him and he reacts in desperation to the ever-tightening trap that is his life. If, as Wilner implies, he defines life through death, then he does so with no sense of possible escape. As evidence for her view she cites his final words—"I'm not dead yet." But like his entire final speech, this line suggests a theatrical, rather than an actual, assertion of will.

But if we reject Wilner's contention that murder for Hesperus dramatizes a perverse version of Romantic individualism, we cannot so easily dismiss the opposite idea. The Romantic longing for fusion with the infinite may, as in the case of Shelley's *Adonais,* take the form of a death wish. Certainly the death wish is frequently encountered in Beddoes's poetry, and we are reminded again and again that such a wish proved to be more than literary for him. But in Shelley death fractures life, which, "like a dome of many-colored glass / Stains the white radiance of Eternity." Therefore one does not merely "seek shelter in the shadow of the tomb"; rather one seeks to join with what

Wordsworth calls the "active universe."[19] In *The Brides' Tragedy* death is simply the great void, and it brings nonbeing, not non-identity.

We have earlier discussed the generic considerations in Beddoes's work; a word must yet be said concerning its designation as tragedy. In his preface to the play Beddoes defines its theme as the "contest of duties and desires" (173). Nine years later in 1831 he defines the "pivot of all tragedy" as the "struggle between the will of man and the moral law of necessity, wh awaits inevitably his past actions" (651), actually an elaboration of his earlier comment on the play.

Essentially, then, Beddoes articulates one version of the classic definition. But while it is possible that some Romantic dramas approach tragedy in this sense, it is clear that *The Brides' Tragedy* does not. The play fails to dramatize the conflict between free will and necessity; Hesperus is a passive, emotionally disoriented (although not insane, as other characters and some critics assume) spiritual bankrupt whose only solution is to negate life. Hence the play cannot validate human strength and dignity, as various kinds of Western tragedies do; rather, it forces us to recognize the already "dark and troubled" vision of its young author.[20] The Romantics, and Beddoes was no exception, often associated tragedy with pathos, melodrama, or simply "serious" drama. But beneath the convention lurks Beddoes's deep, if as yet latent, pessimism.

Dramatic Fragments: "This Araby of Words"

During the three years following the publication of *The Brides' Tragedy* in 1822, Beddoes behaved like a developing dramatist, not like a future medical student and man of science. He produced numerous dramatic fragments, including major portions of two plays, and his letters frequently contain discussions of contemporary and Renaissance drama.[21] His letters (and the earliest extant come from this period) make numerous reference to "a hopeless confusion of new 'first acts,'" as one critic has complained.[22] The release and encouragement produced by the publication of *The Brides' Tragedy* made possible a rich creative period, especially when one considers his active role as a student, his trip to Italy, and his preparations for Germany. Concerning these dramatic projects he was characteristically self-effacing, but his enthusiasm is clear.[23]

Not surprisingly, these "plays" provide a kind of microcosm of Beddoes's career: they are largely fragmentary, they offer extrinsic interest as well as intrinsic value, and they vary widely in quality. Taken as a whole they show Beddoes groping inevitably—although at times almost blindly—toward the gigantic *Death's Jest Book.* In addition to some lyrics to which we will return in chapter 5, the group consists of four clusters of increasingly longer and more coherent works. "The Last Man" (1823–25) involves fragments only, tantalizing though some of them are. "Love's Arrow Poisoned" (1823–25), except for some fragments, exists in a short prose draft. "Torrismond" (1824) consists of one very full first act. Finally, "The Second Brother" (1824–25) is finished through three acts and part of a fourth; it also includes fragments.

As it exists, "Love's Arrow Poisoned" is only a collection of materials for a play: lines, speeches, and images. No plot can be discerned, but the work was apparently meant to include apparent incest, attempted regicide, the personal conflict of father and son, mistaken identity, revenge, and suicide. It would have involved "struggles of fear, remorse & ambition" (521), Beddoes tells us. Character types and names appear which will reappear in later fragments and in *Death's Jest Book,* especially the sinister Ziba, "born in an old ruined century / Three or four doors above the one we live in" (255). By the second fragment it is clear that, as in *The Brides' Tragedy,* love can be realized only in death, "for not externally this love can live, / But in the soul" since "the bower I spoke of is in Paradise" (254, 257). In both style and vision Beddoes has moved beyond *The Brides' Tragedy.* This globe has become a "fat, unwholesome star, / The bald fool-planet, that has men upon it, / And they nickname it 'world' . . . this humpy bastard of the sun" (261). The man who inhabits this star was created by the faultfinder, the satirist of the universe:

> Dost know
> That Momus picked a burnt-out comet up
> From Vulcan's floor, and stuck a man upon it;
> Then, having laught, he flung the wick away,

> And let the insect feed on planet oil:—
> What was't? Man and his ball.
>
> (261)

These lines spoken by Erminia generally represent the satiric tone of the work and specifically establish, in the final fragment, an attack on a nature—"hell-wombed witch"—the very antithesis of Wordsworth's (263).

In the one completed act of "Torrismond" a son is repudiated by his stern father, setting the son's mind on death and power. Torrismond, "whose veins are stretched by passion's hottest wine" and who "ranges and riots headlong through the world" (268), appears to his father as only a vicious wastrel. Yet like Prince Hal he loves his father, and riots only that he might quell his longing for some redeeming love. Far from being debauched, Torrismond is "not at home / In this December world, with men of ice, / Cold sirs and madams" (271). Like one of Byron's heroes he knows the "curse / Of being for a little world too great, / Demanding more than nature has to give." In the central scene of the piece Torrismond meets Veronica in a secluded, moonlit garden, and discovers her deep and idealized love for him. Since he suddenly recognizes his own love in return, redemption should follow. But as in *The Brides' Tragedy,* love seems to thrive only in the "azure secrecy of night" (277), and at any rate Melchior, a courtier nursing some ambiguous wrong, poisons his father against him. All crises in Beddoes's work end in death; the break between father and son leaves Torrismond "cool as an ice-drop in a dead man's eye, / For winter is the season of the tomb, / And that's my country now" (282). The wish to be unborn—a frequent motif in all of Beddoes's major work—is Torrismond's response to his father's distorted view of his character:

> Tear all my life out of the universe,
> Take off my youth, unwrap me of my years,
> And hunt me up the dark and broken past
> Into my mother's womb; there unbeget me;
> For 'till I'm in thy veins and unbegun,
> Or to the food returned which made the blood
> That did make me, no possible lie can ever
> Unroot my feet to thee.
>
> (283)

If he could but "die to the root" he could deny all validity
of life. For a spiritual exile like Torrismond, the "mighty labour
is to die," but in dying "we'll drive in a chariot to our graves,
/ Wheel'd with big thunder, o'er the heads of men" (283).
The act ends with Torrismond's negative will to power.

For Donner, "Torrismond" is essentially complete in one
act; "as it stands, it conforms with the Aristotelian canon."[24]
He also notes the major improvements in characterization, in
dialogue, and in poetry: "phrasing, diction, and blank verse
alike mark the formation of the mature style."[25] Indeed, he
praises the work extravagantly, invoking Aeschylus and arguing
that the garden scene has "all the grace and artifice of a tune
by Mozart."[26] Unquestionably "Torrismond" is, even unfinished, an improvement in its particulars over *The Brides' Tragedy.*
But it is not finished—only stopped—and there is no hint as
to how the plot could be resolved.

"The Second Brother," longest of these experiments, suc-
ceeds no better—despite the bulk. It grinds to a halt just as a
grave-digging scene commences; even Shakespeare-as-muse cannot push the play beyond its wormy impasse. Here Torrismond
has matured into Orazio, and the father-son conflict has become
a conflict between brothers. The new situation retains the sense
of tragic waste in familial struggles, and widens the political
theme only latent in "Torrismond." Orazio, the brother of the
ruling Duke of Ferrara, is like Torrismond a pleasure-seeker,
even a sybarite. And like the earlier protagonist, he is more
than that. But he has put aside Valeria, his loving wife, and
slipped into deep self-gratification; he is a failed Torrismond.
He calls himself the "Lord of Love" (287), but he identifies
even more strongly with Dionysus. We first see him coming
through the street

> Wrapt like Bacchus, in the hide
> Of a specked panther, with his dancing nymphs,
> And torches bright and many, as his slaves
> Had gathered up the fragments of the sun
> That fell just now. Hark! here his music comes.
> (286)

The description is no accident:

From tower and hill, by trump and cannon's voice,
Have I proclaimed myself a deity's son:
Not Alexander's father, Ammon old,
But ivied Bacchus do I call my sire.
Hymn it once more.

(286)

His taste and behavior remind us of Byron's protagonist in
Sardanapalus; like him he seems to hide much behind his apparently single-minded commitment to pleasure.

As the play begins Marcello, the long-absent second brother
of the duke and his heir apparent, returns unrecognized to Ferrara. He thrusts himself in front of Orazio's procession; the
meeting, as one critic has put it, "is in the tonality of death
confronting life, the skeleton or death's head at the scene of
festivity."[27] Marcello demands alms as the beggar he appears
to be. Orazio, however, not only denies his appeal but—recoil-
ing instinctively—utters a repudiation of the missing brother:
"I would deny, outswear, and overreach, / And pass him with
contempt, as I do you" (289). This gratuitous insult sets in
motion the play's action. As Orazio banquets with his followers,
his long-abandoned wife, Valeria (a married version of Torrismond's Veronica), enters and is reunited with her husband.
At the very moment when his empty life is redeemed through
the renewal of his love and the requital of hers, Valeria's father—
and his creditor—comes to turn him out of his palace and rob
him of his wife. He learns that his brother the duke has died
and that Marcello, still in rags, has assumed the throne.

All of this happens in the first crowded act. The remaining
two acts show the development of Marcello's revenge and his
transformation into the tyrant who becomes death-as-sovereign.
Orazio is imprisoned, Ferrara's other nobles are spurned, and
the stage is set for some kind of gothic confrontation in the
cathedral vault at midnight.

The macabre scene that was to have followed is only vaguely
implied; it probably would have included murder and a faked
resurrection of Valeria, who Orazio has been led to believe is
dead. But it is difficult to see how Beddoes could have completed
the play. Three acts have brought us only to the point at which
the one act of "Torrismond" ended, essentially to Marcello's

argument that "Death is the one condition of our life" (313). As projected, the vault scene could mean nothing to Beddoes; for though the pretended victory over death might fool Orazio, it could never fool the author. If imagination were to provide an answer to the eternal question of death, the answer had to be convincing.

There is a rather frenzied quality about the piece, suggesting Beddoes's lack of sureness about his materials and his theme. And while the power of language and poetry in "Torrismond" is extended, the dramatic "realism" of that work is starting to be displaced by Gothic distortion of situations and speech. This distortion is not simply the result of literary imitation (as it is in his juvenilia) but rather a sign of what is for him the break-down of the barriers between life and death, a breakdown that will affect the character of *Death's Jest Book.* Something of that quality is embodied in Marcello's lines alluded to above:

> Death is the one condition of our life:
> To murmur were unjust; our buried sires
> Yielded their seats to us, and we shall give
> Our elbow-room of sunshine to our sons.
> From first to last the traffic must go on;
> Still birth for death. Shall we remonstrate then?
> Millions have died that we might breathe this day:
> The first of all might murmur, but not we.
>
> (313)

However, Beddoes does murmur; more than that, he will make his major creative effort one huge "jest" against an absurd reality that in these lines Marcello accepts so calmly.

Toward *Death's Jest Book*

"I do not intend to finish that 2nd Brother you saw but am thinking of a very Gothic-styled tragedy for w^h I have a jewel of a name—Death's Jest Book" (604). Thus in the failure of "The Second Brother" lies the origin of his great work; as he had so often done before, Beddoes will start over yet again.

Examination of *The Brides' Tragedy* and the dramatic fragments reveals, despite the *apparent* completeness of the published play, an author groping for a creative fulfillment that continues to be elusive. For Beddoes the drama remains compelling; each new start represents a recommitment to the dramatic shape of value and experience. He appears to think—or try to think—in acts. But the dramatic impulse is impeded by conventional theatrical assumptions and, more significantly, by his inability to define theme clearly—to realize his vision. In *The Brides' Tragedy* and in the fragments Beddoes swerves back and forth between concern for plot and his still largely undefined sense of the world.

But from the perspective of *Death's Jest Book* we can recognize the general direction, however confusedly, in which his imagination is moving in these works. On an obvious level, we see characters like Ziba in "Torrismond" and Melchior in "The Second Brother" emerge again in the major work. More important, however, is the way in which the dramatic impulse gradually comes to assume a "satiric" form. Ermina's impassioned speech in "Love's Arrow Poisoned," to which we referred earlier, argues that man is the product of Momus, the god of ridicule. Gradually Beddoes assumes the perspective of the lonely cosmic outcast who—created by the god of jest—assumes the satiric function himself, almost in self-defense.

This is not to argue that *The Brides' Tragedy* or the fragments are satires. Nor is the satiric impulse like that found in Dryden, or even Blake, a poet with whom he has some affinity. Rather, the satiric element, if not the tone—latent here but powerful in *Death's Jest Book*—reminds us of the revolt against a world conceived as absurd, a conception found in Byron and in later nonsatiric writers. It is indicative of Beddoes's remarkable modernity that he should have come to recognize the inescapably problematic nature of human existence, and that his reaction would be, in Wilner's words, the "creation of an essentially absurdist world—grotesque, self-parodying, nihilistic."[28] If Wilner's last term seems an exaggeration, we need only recall the hopelessness in all these pieces: Hesperus, Floribel, and Olivia inhabit a world barren of spiritual growth; Torrismond, his father, and his lover can only be betrayed; Orazio must be destroyed by a man who returns, almost as from the dead, in a totally unreasonable distortion of probability. Moreover, even the best life can be no more than "a brief parenthesis in chaos" (248).

While there are some conventional aspects of satire here—

in his letters and poetry Beddoes clearly scorns the "cold sirs
and madams"—and while one also finds Manfred-like posturing,
the vital element is a serious revolt against the absurdity of an
existence hedged around by death. Marcello is, at moments, a
spokesman for this view, a view formed by the realization of
the tentative and constantly imperiled condition of life:

> Each minute of man's safety he does walk
> A bridge no thicker than his frozen breath
> O'er a precipitous and craggy danger
> Yawning to death.
>
>   (310)

The result of such a realization is a growing desire to destroy
death itself; for even while identifying death with love, Beddoes's imagination searches for a way to subvert it. And if one
cannot "kill" death, one can be "mad and merry" at his "jovial
feast among the worms" (206):

> But while you still are living,
> What say you to some frolic merriment?
> There are two grassy mounds beside the church,
> My husband and my daughter; let us go
> And sit beside them, and learn silence there;
> Even with such guests we'll hold our revelry
> O'er bitter recollections: there's no anguish,
> No fear, no sorrow, no calamity,
> In the deathful catalogue of human pains,
> But we will jest upon 't, and laugh and sing:
> Let pitiful wretches whine for consolation,
> Thank heaven we despair.
>
>   (228)

The "frolic merriment," the "revelry," the ability to "jest upon
't"—all prepare us for his "very Gothic-styled" play, indeed
his "fool's tragedy."

In the works discussed in this chapter we find that Beddoes's
"Araby of words" ranges from the precious ("full of beeish
truth"), through the crisp and trenchant ("I've given myself,
like alms unto an idiot, / To be for nothing squandered"), to
the rough and grotesque ("be his sop-oracles, and suck yellow

truth / Out of the nipple of his jingling pouch").[29] But it is the latter tone that foreshadows *Death's Jest Book*. Here is Marcello as the spectator of death confronting Orazio, whom he likens to love:

> Let us shake hands; I tell thee, brother skeleton,
> We're but a pair of puddings for the dinner
> Of Lady worm; you served in silks and gems,
> I garnished with plain rags. Have I unlocked thee?
>   (288)

It is not surprising to find this example in the last of the fragments; in *Death's Jest Book,* which he is now to begin, the grotesque and satirical will become the dominant tone.

When Beddoes left for Germany in July 1825 the personal isolation he would there assume was, in a sense, symbolic of the social and cosmic alienation he had already come to feel.[30] Whether or not his mother's death played any major role in his darkened vision is unclear; what is obvious is that at twenty-two years old he had none of the youthful optimism warranted by his age, success, and promise. More significantly, instead of the law, which it had apparently been his intention to pursue, he now chose not only his father's medical profession, but the life of the scientist in general. Such a choice reflects a deliberate and major shift; though he might dabble in poetry he would now trust reason over imagination, "prefer Anatomy &c to poetry" (618). While this new dedication partly reveals a lack of self-confidence—"I never cd have been the real thing as a writer" (618)—it chiefly reflects an increasingly desperate attempt to find an alternative avenue to truth.

His faith in the scalpel and microscope seems to have been real enough—at first. He felt, and tried unsuccessfully to explain in his letters, an important conjunction between anatomy and poetry. He chided Kelsall for "having anticipated a regular M.D. to arise" from his ashes after his "reduction in the crucible of German philosophy" (610–11). He now felt that the secret of life and death—the two were for him identical—could be found only by a thinker willing to try all the doors of Keats's "Chamber of Maiden Thought." He was, therefore, "determined never to listen to any metaphysician who is not both anatomist & physiologist of the first rank" (612). In the dissecting room and at his writing table the body—flesh, organs, and especially bones—obsesses his mind. And in Beddoes's Janus-faced search for the bone of Luz, *Death's Jest Book* is born.

Chapter Four

Death's Jest Book
or The Fool's Tragedy:
Satiric Danse Macabre

Death's Jest Book, ready for publication in 1829 but held, like Wordsworth's *Prelude,* for perpetual revision until Beddoes's death, is the liver of his imagination—absorbing and retaining the embittered products of his eccentric sensibility. It is actually Beddoes's own anthology, for in addition to the unique, labyrinthine play, it contains numerous songs and lyrics that are the play's by-products. The work is Beddoes's major accomplishment, a flawed masterpiece, as recent critics have asserted. He had warned his contemporaries against simple imitation and had recognized the need "to give literature of this age an idiosyncrasy & spirit of its own" (595). However indebted to the Jacobeans, Beddoes fulfills in *Death's Jest Book* his own demand.

Beddoes's new play began well enough. In 1825 he wrote a friend about a "very Gothic-styled play" for which he had found "a jewel of a name" (604). He admitted that it would be "a rather quaint and unintelligible tragedy" (605). A year later it was that "never-ending Jest-book" and by 1837 it had "grown deueced grey" (616, 659). But for all his apparent rejection of literature for science he would not abandon the work; whenever he wrote another song he simply found a likely niche and "stuck it into the endless J.B." (674). By 1844 "old J.B., repeatedly touched up, is a strange conglomerate" (676). Two years before his death in 1849 "the unhappy Jestbook," stillborn child of his anguished imagination, remained to haunt his life like one of his many fictional ghosts (679). It had never become the play he had intended it to be.

Indeed, like *The Brides' Tragedy, Death's Jest Book* is marked by the usual Romantic difficulties with drama; it fails to meet structural imperatives, does not maintain sufficiently clear distinctions between characters (i.e., the usual ventriloquism is present) and explores a subject thematically too exotic. The latter quality is heightened by Beddoes's peculiar insularity and obsessions. It may be argued that, like other Romantics, Beddoes attempted drama with the equipment of a writer of dramatic lyrics. Yet what one sees in *Death's Jest Book* (as one sees in Byron's self-styled "metaphysical" plays or in what he called his "mental theatre")[1] is the only partially understood need for a new dramatic form, a manifestation of the larger crisis of genre experienced by many major writers in the nineteenth century.

As it exists, *Death's Jest Book* is the culmination of many abortive dramatic experiments and must be discussed in terms of its own unique generic nature, in the same sense that *The Marriage of Heaven and Hell, The Prelude,* and *Don Juan* must be so considered. Its dramatic failings—if that is the correct way to describe them—negate neither the lyrical brilliance of the poetry nor the characteristic somber gaiety and mordant wit of his grotesque vision. "In it Despair has married wildest mirth," Beddoes claimed (614), and Robert Browning agreed, one of the first to recognize the interpenetration of the comic and tragic as the essence of Beddoes's poetry.[2]

Whatever the case with Beddoes's earlier drama, in *Death's Jest Book,* death has ceased to be only the cliché of popular Gothic horror, or the basic device of Jacobean drama. It has become an ever-varying metaphor for a new and more despairing Romantic vision. Some may question Northrop Frye's description of the play as "a precursor of the theatre of the absurd,"[3] suggesting as it does a clear identification of Beddoes with such moderns as Samuel Beckett. But Frye is certainly correct in finding in Beddoes one aspect of Romanticism, the radical despair, the sense of cosmic alienation and human limitation that would, eventually, elide into an existential view of life. In *Death's Jest Book* the world for Beddoes has become a "hoary atheistic murderous star"; "Nature's polluted, / There's a man in every secret corner of her" (413). It is this vision, along with the Romantic anti-Aristotelian attitude toward form, that explains the oddly modern quality of the play. No well-made play of years to come could possibly be so suggestive of drama's ultimate directions as Beddoes's work.

Moreover, in *Death's Jest Book* we encounter, however peculiar, Romantic mythopoeic poetry; here Beddoes's vision of death as negative apocalyptic realization is completely dramatized.

"The Exact Location of the Soul": Poet as Scientist

More than any of his other works, *Death's Jest Book* finds its stimulus in and takes its character from Beddoes's experience as a scientist. At the level of simplistic generalization, a Romantic antagonism toward science has often been simply taken for granted. A widespread Romantic reassessment of the value of imagination and a corresponding attack on mechanical reason (and on the "universe of death" it was felt to have produced) partly account for this assumption. There is, moreover, Blake's impressive assault on "Newton's sleep,"[4] and Keats's argument (Keats with Lamb drank a well-known toast to the "confusion of mathematics") that "all charms fly / At the mere touch of cold philosophy" (science) which would "unweave a rainbow."[5] Yet Keats was not representative; Shelley could speak of "Science, and her sister Poesy," who would "clothe in light the fields and cities of the free," and spend his only term at Oxford conducting experiments in his room.[6] Coleridge and Wordsworth had been acquaintances of the senior Dr. Beddoes and interested visitors at his Pneumatical Institute. Natural philosophy intrigued many contemporaries—however much they might share Coleridge's concept of the organic unity of all mental faculties. And Coleridge's theory of mental unity might actually have helped Beddoes, whose own epistemology was to become increasingly bifurcated.

Presumably an anatomist studies the structure, not the source and secret, of life; he might even be accused of "murdering to dissect." Certainly Beddoes's radical, rationalistic inheritance, combined with the practical possibilities of German medicine and reinforced by his own sense of artistic inferiority, now produced a skeptical attitude toward poetry and the role of poet. Beddoes's comments cited earlier, which seem to denigrate poetry, probably emerge from this nexus. Yet for Beddoes, anatomy—and related medical sciences—seemed to offer a means

of reaching the "bone of Luz,"[7] the philosopher's stone, a way
to discover the vital spark so long the metaphorical province
of art, religion, even magic.

He could argue, as we have seen, that the roles of physician
and dramatist are very similar. "Apollo has been barbarously
separated by the Moderns," he argued, and he "would endeavor
to unite him" (611). At the outset of his German experience
he seems to have been content to pursue his new scientific studies, perhaps confident that the microscope and dissecting table
would carry him to the kind of knowledge he had hoped to
find with his poetry. Then he might have agreed with Thoreau
when the latter urged us not to "underrate the value of a fact;
it will one day flower in a truth" if given the opportunity by
the scientist whose imaginative powers are equal to his skill at
rational analysis.[8] But his precise hopes for medicine, as for
poetry earlier, seem vague, and the eventual failure of the former only helped to undercut the latter.

Unable to discover the essence behind the material he was,
in fact, a vivid example of the fact-value schism that so troubled
the nineteenth-century mind and remains to trouble our own.
Beddoes was a highly gifted student of science, but anatomy
could lead him only farther into despair. The American surgeon
Richard Selzer also claims to "seek the soul in the facts of animal
economy and progligancy"; it is "the exact location of the soul"
for which he probes the human body. "In the recesses of the
body I search for the philosophers' stone. I know it is there,
hidden in the deepest, dampest cul-de-sac. . . . To find it would
be like the harnessing of fire." But repeatedly Selzer finds that
the "surprise at the center of his work . . . is death," not the
bone of Luz, which Beddoes longed, if not expected, to find.[9]
However painful, this realization seems to remain an acceptable
mystery to Selzer. For Beddoes, however, it was an agony that
neither his Romantic imagination nor his father's rationalism
could subdue.

Such, then, is the background out of which *Death's Jest Book,*
his major creation, emerges. Relocation to the Continent gave
a nomadic reality to his restless, Faustian mind—already a spiritual wanderer. If the roles of physician and dramatist were similar, the similarity lay in their goals, not their epistemologies.
Though he would try, he was never to reunite Apollo's roles

as god of medicine and poetry. Eventually, claiming to be "essentially unpoetical in character," he would declare his "preference of Apollo's pill box to his lyre" and "Göttingen instead of Grub street" (636). He came to believe that "a man must have an exclusive passion for his art" (647).

Perhaps, had Beddoes been able to dedicate himself utterly to science, these assertions would have been valid. But troubled as he was by his own sense of creative inadequacy—an inadequacy intensified by his friends' critical reception of *Death's Jest Book*—he remains fatally drawn to poetry. Repudiate his calling as he might, his letters long retain mention of publishing projects, however offhanded they may sound, and the attending physician said that even when he was near death, Beddoes still hoped to see his works printed. Aware of his obscurity, he even considered publishing at his own expense. He could neither complete nor dismiss *Death's Jest Book:* "and so I weave my Penelopean web and rip it up again: and so I roll my impudent Sisyphean stone" (666).

But like the rest of Beddoes's poetry, *Death's Jest Book* is remarkably free, for the most part, from the general scientific imagery his involvement might have induced. In this respect it is quite unlike the work of his much-admired Shelley, whose interest in science had none of the desperation it had for Beddoes. The absence may seem odd, but for Shelley science provided metaphors for an expansive, speculative vision; for Beddoes only anatomy would suffice to express the quality of his dark vision. Thus when he played "truant from the odd old bones / And winds of flesh," freed for the moment from "Anatomy the grim," reality became metaphor (613, 614).

The Penelopean Web

Beddoes's "Penelopean web," his "Sisyphean stone," is huge, sprawling, yet never quite chaotic. By 1829 it had taken its general form; Beddoes's endless unraveling and reknitting shifted its nuances but did not alter its story line. Set at the end of the thirteenth century (at the start of the fourteenth in revision), the major action takes place in Ancona, Egypt, and Silesia. With the exception of the third act, which has three, each of the five acts fills out four scenes.

Act 1 opens in a tavern on the shore at Ancona. From a discussion between the zany Mandrake and a barmaid we quickly learn part of the story line; the knight Wolfram is ready to sail for Egypt in order to rescue Duke Melveric of Münsterberg, who has been lost on a pilgrimage to the Holy Sepulcher. Torwald, governing in Melveric's absence, mentions important letters for the duke concerning the rivalry of his two sons Adalmar and Athulf, a rivalry that endangers the state. Conversation between Isbrand and Wolfram establishes the main plot; the two are brothers who had originally returned to court—the first as fool, the second as knight—in order to avenge their father's loss of throne and life at the hands of Melveric. But Wolfram has come to love and serve the usurper and now refuses Isbrand's demands that he use the opportunity to destroy their enemy. Isbrand, the self-styled "tragic fool," vows to act alone.

The remaining three scenes of act 1 take place in Egypt, where Melveric, escaped from his captors, awaits rescue by a Christian ship. He in turn has rescued Sibylla, a young woman of unknown origin who, though she believes herself in love with the duke, recalls the profound feelings produced in her by a Saxon knight, a man we later discover to have been Wolfram. When Wolfram and his knights arrive, Melveric at once makes clear his intense love for Sibylla and his refusal to recognize any other's claim, even that of his best friend. The two parties separate and, even after Melveric attempts to poison Wolfram through the duke's slave Ziba, Wolfram returns to save his life during the duke's attack by Arabs. Wolfram is repaid by a mortal wound from Melveric's sword; however, he refuses to betray his murderer to Sibylla, who was not present when they fought. Melveric has killed his truest friend, one with whom he had made a blood pact that the first to die would return to visit the other.

Act 2 returns us to Ancona, where Melveric leaves the dead knight with an order for his honorable funeral, and the grief-stricken Sibylla with a curiously perfunctory offer of refuge. He departs for the capital disguised as a pilgrim, a disguise he maintains until near the play's end. After his departure, Isbrand and his accomplice Siegfried force the terrified Mandrake to pose as the dead Wolfram, whose body they carry off, intending it for burial in the duke's chapel in Silesia. Isbrand dedicates himself to the destruction of the duke and his sons; to achieve this end he will become "Death the Court-fool."

At the ducal castle an exchange between the two princes indicates a serious conflict of character and motive; both love the governor Torwald's daughter Amala. Melveric reveals his true identity to Torwald, who in turn discloses a plot against his throne. Isbrand confides to Siegfried his conviction that Melveric murdered Wolfram, and he alludes to his own major role in the impending revolt. He also tells of his substitution in the duke's crypt of Wolfram for the duke's long-dead wife; once buried, Melveric will find himself "embracing his damnation."

In act 3 we learn that Amala, despite her impending marriage to Adalmar, loves his brother Athulf. The action shifts to the ruins of a Gothic cathedral. The final long scene opens with Mandrake speculating, in a very amusing soliloquy, on the "fictitious condition" of death; he is living in the sepulcher. The conspirators, including the still-disguised duke, assemble. When the group has left, Ziba offers Melveric, now deeply grieving for his dead wife, buried in these ruins, the opportunity to recall her from the dead. Torwald arrives to protest such a desecration, and the attempt is postponed until after Isbrand and Siegfried have arrived and left. Though depressed at his sons' disloyalty and longing for his wife, Melveric is skeptical of Ziba's powers and reminds the slave of his own broken pact with Wolfram who—though murdered by his friend and therefore doubly motivated—has failed to return. Confident of his powers, Ziba makes the attempt; however, it is Mandrake who first answers his summons. While Melveric reels under this terrible joke, Wolfram, substituted for the duke's wife by Isbrand, obeys the order.

Act 4 opens on the following morning, a badly shaken Melveric consulting with Torwald on plans to thwart the threatened rebellion. He reveals himself to his son Adalmar, promising to be available when his son needs him. In a garden Wolfram seeks out the desolate Sibylla and woos his former lover; she, solemn but joyous, promises to return with him to the world of the dead.

Beneath Amala's window Athulf, torn between despair and thoughts of fratricide, confronts his brother's intended bride with his own tormented love. When she leaves after urging him to forget her, he drinks poison secured from Ziba. While waiting to die he is discovered by Adalmar, who declares his suicide to be self-damnation, and who, when he discovers the poison's source, leaves to find the antidote. Amala returns to find Athulf apparently dying; before leaving she promises, like Sibylla, to return to her true lover in death. When the poison is discovered to be a harmless drug, Athulf stabs his brother, his murder the second such betrayal in the play.

This act concludes with a triumphant scene in the hall of the ducal castle; the city appears to have been subdued by Isbrand's conspirators. Ziba, loyal to Melveric, attempts to kill Isbrand, fails, and is spared. Left alone, Isbrand reveals his aspiration not only for the throne but for transcendence itself.

The play's final act opens with a short scene in which Isbrand speculates on the "bit of Fiat" in his soul with which he will "create" his "little world." Siegfried informs the others of Isbrand's growing egomania and admits his desire to see the old duke return.

The final scene, again set in the ruined cathedral, opens with figures from the dance of death descending from the wall to sing and mock the victory feast Isbrand has planned to hold there. When the major characters arrive on stage, Wolfram attends them as court fool. He reveals Ziba's plan to poison Isbrand on behalf of Siegfried, and the latter is seized. Dragged away, he wishes them all "happily old, mad, sick and dead, and cursed." As Sibylla's funeral train passes, Mario, a blind advocate of liberty, stabs Isbrand. While the dying court fool struggles against his mortality, Melveric is restored to his dukedom. Isbrand dies, but before Melveric can celebrate his restoration Amala enters, followed by the bier of Adalmar. Athulf arrives, accepts his guilt, and stabs himself to death. Melveric surrenders his newly regained throne and is summoned by Wolfram "still alive, into the world o'th'dead."

Faithful to the main action, the preceding outline can hardly represent the play's unique character, which should emerge more clearly in the remainder of this chapter. Such a description rationalizes the action, suggesting a level of "realism" that does not actually exist, either in the portrayal of characters or in the structured behavior of those characters. Nor can it more than hint at the extraordinary tone, mood, and atmosphere.

However, in general the play can be described as theatrically more operatic than dramatic, more symbolic than representational.

The Dialogue of the Mind with Itself

Beddoes wrote *The Brides' Tragedy,* he said, "exclusively for the closet" (172); in contrast he several times indicated his intention to see *Death's Jest Book* acted. He certainly knew a great deal about the theater, especially the Renaissance drama, which his work so strongly, if superficially, resembles. Yet it is clear that a contemporary audience, had the play ever reached the boards, would have been at the very least disappointed. Despite the heavy melodrama such an audience enjoyed, despite the tendency toward stock character types so typical of accepted theatrical practice, the play is unlikely to have been successful. Not only is it very long but, more important, it lacks the kind of plot the audience of his age would have expected. Moreover, his characters are not what they appear to be.

In fact, the play's tendency toward stock characterization is misleading. Normally in drama unindividualized characters exist to serve the purpose of plot since, traditionally at least, action is dominant. Yet in *Death's Jest Book* plot has a curiously muted, secondary quality. The above summary of the play would seem to belie this fact; we discover fights, murders, comic and serious resurrections. And there is, it is true, a sequence of events that leads to a radical change in the play's original world. But these events seem somehow to lack the mandate of causal pattern; even Beddoes, in 1826, saw the play's parts "as scattered and unconnected" (620). They appear to be more important as a background against which one or two characters work out their fragmented personalities, rather than as a part of some clearly defined structural whole. It is not that the "dominance of narrative hindered development of dramatic forms," as Karl Kroeber has said;[10] it is the dominance of a peculiarly symbolic kind of character over action.

Even the Romantics themselves understood why this should be so. George Darley was concerned that "subjective composition" was the "natural tendency" of his "refined age," but he recognized that subjectivity might be useful to the writer. The

problem occurs when the subjective "poetry of experience"[11]—
poetry that explores rather than asserts truth—is put into an
objective form. Aristotle had seen the center of drama in its
mimetic character, hence in plot. What Matthew Arnold
mourned (a Romantic poet with classical convictions) was the
shift from the "calm, the cheerfulness, the disinterested objectiv-
ity" to "modern problems"; he lamented being forced to witness
the "dialogue of the mind with itself" in the Hamlets and
Fausts.[12] His reference to Hamlet reminds us of Coleridge's
influential criticism written on that protomodern character, and
mention of Faust locates us squarely in the tradition of Romantic
drama. It is character, not action, that emerges there as the
imaginative center; Faust, Manfred, and Beddoes's Isbrand all
serve their authors as modes of very personal exploration and
expression. As Terry Otten reminds us, in this sense Romantic
poetry "is nearly always dramatic because it is both dialectical
and dynamic."[13] But such drama is not conventionally theatrical,
and insofar as the Romantic dramatist attempted to subordinate
the dialogue of the mind with itself to the most objective of
literary forms, the fatal generic flaw was produced.

Despite good arguments to the contrary, Byron's intention
to write for the "mental theatre" was more than sour grapes;
it was an attempt at a new literary, if not dramatic, form. However slavish an imitator he might appear in his "neoclassical"
plays, in his self-styled "metaphysical" drama he sought a form
appropriate to the acute self-consciousness he shared with his
age, and with modern poetry in general. Beddoes, however,
was so deeply committed to the communal drama of Shakespeare
that he continually attempted to subordinate his own personal,
subjective, exploratory vision to the grand dramatic design. He
was so immersed in Renaissance drama that the result was a
deceptively good imitation, hence the error of such perceptive
critics as Lytton Strachey in taking him too seriously as "the
last Elizabethan." This error is very like the one made by critics
who attempt to explain Byron's *Don Juan* in terms of traditional
satire; in both cases the choice of genre obscures the actual
imaginative goals.

The issue here is the degree to which Beddoes is a poet of
experience. Is the play assertive or exploratory? To what degree
is it question rather than answer? The weakness of many good

rhetorical and thematic analyses alike results from ignoring the fluid, pragmatic, tentative nature of the work. As a scientist and as a poet he approached the problem of life-death empirically, and as an artist he sought the epiphany, not the symbolic expression of a formulated concept. Beddoes's poetry is, therefore, not a celebration but rather a continual form of realization; as process it can give a fluid, organic form, not a traditional rhetorical structure. *Death's Jest Book* is an instrument on which Beddoes can practice a sort of sustained improvisation; the form is thus characteristically modern. As the result of process it can be obsessive yet fragmentary, vivid yet illusive, profoundly felt, yet tentatively understood. As John Gardner has recently reminded us, "art, in sworn opposition to chaos, discovers *by its process* what it can say."[14]

Thus dramatic *Death's Jest Book* is, but dramatic in the sense that the play becomes a great stage on which Beddoes can act out, explore, and assess all his feelings and ideas, a place where he can test approaches to life through role playing, a means of articulating his troubled vision. It is dramatic, then, in the same sense as *Faust* and *Manfred,* which is to say *monodramatic.* In a rough sort of way the characters are Beddoes himself exploded into his several parts: the women tender and passive; the jester bitter, brilliant, outraged, outrageous; the zany genuinely comic and spiritually healthy; the duke steely, detached, secretly longing for redeeming love. Wolfram is Beddoes's better part but blunted, vague, uncertain. Isbrand is, perhaps, his darker side, yet active, Faustian, strong-willed—a spokesman for all the existential, emotional, even cosmic rage that Beddoes's letters carefully conceal. Hence the stylized appearance of his characters, and the critical error in judging them by standards of typical dramatic development, or even moral consistency. Wagner argues that Beddoes's characters have "the essential unity of dream characters." He sees them meeting "in the dreamer" and calls them "emanations of the central idea."[15] The dreamer, then, is Beddoes.

Just as Beddoes succumbed to pressure from his own idiosyncratic imagination and unconsciously, perhaps, attempted to make drama the vehicle for that subjective perspective, so his sense of the world's radical disorder played a part in his transformation of the genre as well. The world of *King Lear* is brutally disrupted by Lear's acts; the very weather on the heath reflects its disorder. But at the play's conclusion order, however wan, is reestablished; the drama is intended to reassert that social and cosmic pattern against which the tragedy takes place and indeed makes Lear's experience tragic in the first place. But for Beddoes there is no longer any such order to dissolve and re-create dramatically; his drama—ironically the very genre licensed by belief in order—portrays the chaotic nature of human experience. It is for this reason that Northrop Frye likens *Death's Jest Book* to the drama of the absurd. Since there is no horizon of intelligibility in Beddoes's world, there can be only his perception, along with the artist's need to give a meaningful shape to the articulation of that perception of unintelligibility. However much he may have wished to publish or stage *Death's Jest Book,* the driving force behind his work is his prior need to express—despite, or even perhaps because of, his failure to achieve some meaningful closure.

Satiric Pathos

Prevented from approaching *Death's Jest Book* by means of conventional dramatic criticism we may initially stand baffled before its complexities. But even one reading makes clear the need to consider the play's tone; Beddoes's attitude toward the characters' multiple arguments and contradictory behavior can best be reached through an understanding of this peculiar quality.

In 1851 Henry Crabbe Robinson, that tireless observer of English authors, noted with interest the presence in *Death's Jest Book* of horror in "grotesque combination with comedy."[16] Seventeen years later Robert Browning claimed to "see what Beddoes wanted to do, and what effect he aimed at in this interfusion of the 'comic stuff' Milton objects to when blent with 'Tragic sadness & gravity,'" and he lamented that Beddoes's comic faculty had not been developed "equally with the tragic power."[17] Most critics since that time have been impressed, as is Harold Bloom, by the "almost playful" quality of Beddoes's work; and writers generally share G. Wilson Knight's feeling that *Death's Jest Book* is "ghoulish, yet merry."[18] Beddoes argued for the mixed tone of English drama in the play's preface: "some-

times light and joyous, sometimes fearfully hideous—often satirical, grotesque or ludicrous" (534). These impressions are
justified, but misleading. Though there are moments of exuberant comedy in the play—especially those associated with Mandrake, the zany—the prevailing humor is black, not comic, and
Beddoes's "tragic power," evident not only to Browning but
to many modern commentators as well, is insufficient to transcend it. Beddoes himself complained of "some wretched comic
parts in it, w^h I cannot improve nor give up" (639). That he
"sports and mocks among the grim creatures of his fancy"[19]
and thereby reduces or alters the Gothic and Jacobean horror
to something quite different, is true. But the comedy of *Death's
Jest Book* in no sense possesses the life-affirming qualities we
associate with the traditional mode. The nature and tone of
the work are produced by a shift from what he now has come
to call "Parnassian foolery" to a darker, more sardonic mode;
if lyrical celebration and tragic grandeur are now impossible,
he can "bear a satire still tho' and write one, as Jest-Book shall
show. . . . It is anatomy that works in me so wittily" (619).

Beddoes's early references to the play in his letters suggest
mainly its tragic character—it will be a "very Gothic-styled tragedy" (604)—and among other dramas, Shelley's tragedy *The
Cenci* is much on his mind. But in a verse epistle to Procter
early in 1826, Beddoes's intentions, which had been gradually
shifting, become more clearly defined. Whenever freed from
his "rulling spright / Anatomy the grim" he turned to his new
work, "in whose satiric pathos we will glory" (614). Satiric
pathos is achieved when "Despair has married wildest mirth"
(614). And who will be the "fool o' the feast" (614) at their
wedding banquet? His answer deserves quoting in full, for it
suggests so powerfully both the extraordinary significance to
Beddoes of *Death's Jest Book,* as well as the risk he was taking:

> I've dug him up and decked him trim
> And made a mock, a fool, a slave of him
> Who was the planet's tyrant: dotard death:
> Man's hate and dread: not with a stoical breath
> To meet him like Augustus standing up,
> Nor with grave saws to season the cold cup
> Like the philosopher nor yet to hail

His coming with a verse or jesting tale
As Adrian did and More: but of his night
His moony ghostliness and silent might
To rob him, to un-cypress him i' the light
To unmask all his secrets; make him play
Momus o'er wine by torchlight is the way
To conquer him and kill; and from the day
Spurned hissed and hooted send him back again
An unmasked braggart to his bankrupt den.
For death is more "a jest" than Life: you see
Contempt grows quick from familiarity.
I owe this wisdom to Anatomy—

(614–15)

We have seen earlier his conviction that the "man who is
to awaken the drama must be a bold trampling fellow," one
who could give his age its own "idiosyncracy & spirit" (595).
But as Northrop Frye reminds us, to treat death as no greater
a threat than a *miles gloriosus* demanded a spiritual optimism
beyond most modern writers, but infinitely beyond Beddoes.[20]
These lines contain a note of desperate bravado; not even in
his most idealistic moments does he arrive at the point where
either poetry or science seems to offer such a potential victory
over the source of his obsession.

But he does intend a satire. In fact, the key to his new state
of mind can be found in the same verse epistle when, after
boldly asserting the program described above, he contrasts Procter's gentler muse with his own: "Few I know, / Can bear to
sit at my board when I show / The wretchedness and folly of
man's all / And laugh myself right heartily. Your call / Is higher
and more human: I will do / Unsociably my part & still be
true / To my own soul" (615). While the note of confidence
is seemingly retained here, a sense of isolation has emerged,
the loneliness of all scourgers of human folly—that eternal target
of satirists. And from this point on the letters are marked increasingly by the satirical perspective; for several years his letters
will burn with resentment at such varied aspects of life as the
"mental stagnation of Europe," the wretched "windeggs" of
German tragedy, the "invincible insular self-complacency" of
the English, even "the old pig of Weimar," Goethe (616, 621,
626, 631). It is not simply that "the tragic view of life gives

way to the melodramatic," as John Heath-Stubbs argues,[21] but rather that it largely yields to the satiric; and the satiric view will give way to that of the absurdist, the role often forced on the modern satirist.

"Dissatisfaction is the lot of the poet, if it be that of any being," Beddoes claimed in 1827, and "to annoy and puzzle the fools and amuse oneself with their critical blunders" is the only justification for publishing, "excepting poverty, Mr. Croly: excepting avarice, Sir Walter" (635). But we must be careful not to confuse the dissatisfaction of the traditional satirist with that which more and more possessed Beddoes. Whereas Dryden might seize upon the same "wretchedness and folly," his use of it would be fundamentally different. For Dryden or Pope, aberrant behavior simply demanded reformation. Whatever may be said about the satirical temperament, eighteenth-century satire brought with it its own rationale; it assumed a community of shared values against which to measure negative behavior. Writers often used medical imagery, as Dryden does here, to describe the satirist's responsibility to society: "He who writes Honestly, is no more an Enemy to the Offendour, than the Physician to the Patient, when he prescribes harsh Remedies to an inveterate Disease; for those, are only in order to prevent the Chyrurgeon's work of an Ense rescindendum, which I wish not to my very Enemies. To conclude all, if the Body Politique have any Analogy of the Natural, in my weak judgment, an Act of Oblivion were as necessary in a Hot, Distemper'd State, as an Opiate woud be in a Raging Fever."[22]

The fact of illness implies the possibility of health, and in this sense traditional satire is optimistic, even idealistic. With a firm faith in a stable world, the writer could believe with Dryden that "the true end of Satyre, is the amendment of Vices by correction."[23]

Beddoes, however, could diagnose but offer no cure for the "inveterate disease." Like Matthew Arnold he had come to know the "sick fatigue, the languid doubt"; he had laid bare Arnold's "strange disease of modern life."[24] But the traditional metaphor of the satirist-as-healer has become only the "pleasure of dissecting & laughing at" some distortion of the accepted norm (618). He had left the comfortable world of Procter's normal muse for an extreme state wherein the poet necessarily

murdered to dissect; the satire of *Death's Jest Book* is that of
the anatomist flaying the flesh from the human head to reveal
the lipless grin of a Yorick beneath.

The reason for such a radical shift is not difficult to determine.
By the middle and late 1820s the concomitant failure of Beddoes's science and poetry—reason and imagination—appeared
to him inevitable. Near the end of a long letter to Kelsall he
mentions his plans to publish "an inquiry into the laws of the
Growth & Restoration in organized matter" (629). Then, quite
suddenly, he shifts mood and tone but not really topic:

I am now already so thoroughly penetrated with the conviction of
the absurdity & unsatisfactory nature of human life that I search with
avidity for every shadow of a proof or probability of an after-existence,
both in the material & immaterial nature of man. Those people, perhaps
they are few, are greatly to be envied who believe, honestly and
from conviction, in the Xtian doctrines: but really in the New T. it
is difficult to scrape together hints for a doctrine of immortality. Man
appears to have found out this secret for himself, & it is certainly
the best part of all religion and philosophy, the only truth worth
demonstrating: an anxious question full of hope & fear & promise,
for w^h Nature appears to have appointed one solution—Death. In
times of revolution & business, and even now, the man who can lay
much value in the society, praise, or glory of his fellows, may forget,
and he who is of a callous phlegmatic constitution may never find
the dreadful importance of the doubt. (629–30)

"Absurdity" and "doubt"—there it is. This letter of October
1827 is the first sustained expression of his growing pessimism
concerning the validity of life itself. Nor is it simply undergraduate posturing or ennui; we hear the tone of genuine despair—
quiet and dignified. It is not, therefore, "value in the society"
that concerns him—that fragile structure flung out over the
abyss—but the fundamental question about life, which only
death could answer. What "but an after life can . . . quench
the greediness of the spirit for existence" (630), he asks rhe-
torically, and what but death offers the key to that state after
one has exhausted the "material & immaterial nature of man"
by one's science and art? *Death's Jest Book* was originally intended
to be his organized assault on man's fundamental ignorance,
an attempt through "satiric pathos" to make death yield the
truth of its nature, and reveal its fraudulent claims on life. Bed-

does "deliberately attempted to defeat death," as Wagner says, by "creating a fantastic world where humour was equivalent to reason."[25]

In his attempt Beddoes experienced the dilemma of the modern satirist. However, his difficulty was not like that of William Blake, who in *The Marriage of Heaven and Hell* had to find a way to satirize readers with whom he shared no values and simultaneously offer them an alternative, healthy vision. Rather, he was closer to Byron (for whom he had contempt); unable to accept society's values, and lacking positive alternatives, both writers experienced the nihilism that would become so much a part of the modern attitude. Hence, in Geoffrey Wagner's words, Beddoes's "whole satire is a form of retaliation against a society he so despised."[26] In *Don Juan* Byron was at least able to attack society for its failure to live by its own values, thus providing an outlet for his satirical impulse. The problem for Beddoes, however, was more extreme; he could not focus on social behavior itself.

The absence of a positive worldview does not prevent the longing for surety. In attempting to explain and justify Cain's behavior, Byron speaks of the first murderer's "rage and fury against the inadequacy of his state to his conceptions."[27] Albert Camus would later find the source of the absurd precisely in "the mind that desires and the world that disappoints."[28] It is this same inability to bridge the gap that increasingly lies behind Beddoes's nightmare vision. Man may "have found out this secret [of immortality] for himself," but Beddoes, despite his enormous desire, has been personally unable to achieve that end. Hence his satire can be cathartic neither in the traditional social nor the personal sense; hence unable "to conquer . . . and kill" death, Beddoes turns the jest against the absurdity of life itself. The latent satirical impulse we have seen in his earlier work has fully emerged, and lacking an alternative, the grotesque—already evident in *The Improvisatore* and *The Brides' Tragedy*—now becomes central to his vision.

Isbrand

Death's Jest Book opens with the zany Homunculus Mandrake planning to leave for Egypt, there to search for the philosopher's stone. The zany is, of course, a stock character in old comedies—

absurd, ludicrous, possibly a complete buffoon—and his traditional role, therefore, would have been attractive to Beddoes.
But even more important, here his quest is an obvious self-
parody on Beddoes's part and suggests that the satire in *Death's
Jest Book* is directed at himself as well as the world. Before
leaving, he pauses to regret the decline of his profession; "we
are laid aside and shall soon be forgotten . . . now is every
man his own fool, and the world's cheerless" (328). Isbrand,
to whom he makes this observation, remarks that Mandrake
"commencest philosopher, and then thou art only a fellow-ser-
vant out of livery" (330); in this play, as generally in the Renaissance tradition, the fool is linked with knowledge and wisdom.
The comic Mandrake prepares us for the satiric Isbrand, who,
when he learns of his brother's death, promises to "jest more
merrily than now: for I shall be Death the Court-fool" (402).

Isbrand probably had originally been designed as a conventional satiric device to make a "mock, a fool, a slave of . . .
the planet's tyrant: dotard Death," as Beddoes had promised
in his verse letter to Procter; *Death's Jest Book* was intended
to do the impossible. But at the play's conclusion, Isbrand, mor-
tally wounded by a fellow conspirator, admits that "now Death
makes indeed a fool of me" (485). Immediately following Isbrand's death Wolfram invites down from the wall the painted
deaths "to present masque and dance" to the survivors of the
rebellion (485). When these figures descend to "celebrate
Death's harvest-Home," Wolfram describes their performance
as the play's "antimasque, / I think they call it; 'tis satirical"
(485). Indeed it is; in the increasingly surrealistic atmosphere
of the last act, death and his dancers have the last jest, and it
is appropriate that Wolfram, acting as court jester after his resurrection, sets the fool's cap back on Isbrand's head. The play is
truly Death's jest book; starting as a satire destructive of death,
the play has turned into death's own satire on the jest of life
itself. This reversal represents the poetic process we have seen
at work in Romantic poetry and, as such, it is a painful reminder
of the discoveries Beddoes was forced to make and poetically
acknowledge.

Beddoes had clearly failed to achieve his original intention
in the play—to make death a dotard. As Browning noted, "how
curiously different it proves from that which is announced, and

probably believed in, by Beddoes in his letter of verse to Procter: he was to despoil Death of his terrors, strip him of his dart, & so on—make him the 'fool of the feast': he does exactly the reverse." But it is not true, as Browning goes on to insist, that the play actually heightens our fear of death in the manner of so many medieval devices.[29] Rather, the satirical tone often takes the form of what Snow calls a "reckless and distorted gaiety"[30]—a kind of exuberant grief—and creates a climate of bitter intellectual analysis. In other words, the satire of death becomes of necessity a satire of life itself.

Before Isbrand falls as a result of overreach, he becomes the chief spokesman for this attitude. It is the jester who is at the heart of the play's ironical view of human existence. In a world devoid of value and inescapably in the grip of death, absurdity is all that remains to be portrayed. And if death itself is out of reach, the world of fools who fail to recognize this absurdity remains to be satirized.

"The fool . . . signifies humanity," Mandrake says early in the revised first act, suggesting, as do his previously quoted lines, the inversion of knowledge in Beddoes's world: "now is every man his own fool" (328, 329). In turn the fool, the jester, the court clown represents genuine understanding—a realization of the discrepancy between human awareness and the irrationality of a universe in which death is the only important fact. Duke Melveric, in despair over his sons' defection, expresses the play's general attitude toward earthly existence:

> Nature's polluted,
> There's man in every secret corner of her,
> Doing damned wicked deeds. Thou art old, world,
> A hoary atheistic murderous star:
> I wish that thou would'st die, or could'st be slain,
> Hell-hearted bastard of the sun.
>
> (413)

Isbrand also believes that "the world's man-crammed; we want no more of them" (436). Beddoes the scientist has become, in the character of Ziba, a sinister child of death who really does know the secret of the "seed-shaped bone, / Aldabaron, called by the Hebrews Luz" but this dubious source of resur-

rection can produce only "the bloody, soul-possessed weed
called man" (436). Life is a bad joke played on this wretched
creature, since "nothing's true / But what is horrible" (444).
Attempting to protect himself from obvious but trivial dangers,
man fails to see the real threat to his brief and fragile tenure.
As a physician, Beddoes know that if

> man could see
> The perils and diseases that he elbows,
> Each day he walks a mile; which catch at him,
> Which fall behind and graze him as he passes;
> Then would he know that Life's a single pilgrim,
> Fighting unarmed amongst a thousand soldiers.
>   (444)

However, not only is physical existence threatened; more important, a radical instability in human nature itself produces a world
without moral or even rational center, a subject to which we
will return later in this chapter.

The conventional responsibility of the fool-as-satirist, therefore, no longer has any meaning. Isbrand, after a traditional
sally against the court, declares that he

will now speak a word in earnest, and hereafter jest with you no
more: for I lay down my profession of folly. Why should I wear
bells to ring the changes of your follies on? Doth the besonneted
moon wear bells, she that is the parasite and zany of the stars, and
your queen, ye apes of madness? As I live I grow ashamed of the
duality of my legs, for they and the apparel, forked or furbelowed,
upon them constitute humanity; the brain no longer; and I wish I
were an honest fellow of four shins when I look into the notebook
of your absurdities. I will abdicate. (405)

Indeed, Isbrand is in earnest in this speech, which repeats
the comic assertion with which Mandrake opens the play. This
passage and the following one are spoken in act 2 before Isbrand's search for revenge becomes the reckless obsession of
an existential overreacher. At this point rage at the injustice
of his brother's murder provokes lines central to our understanding of the play:

I will yield Death the crown of folly. He hath no hair, and in this
weather might catch cold and die: besides he has killed the best knight

I knew, Sir Wolfram, and so is doubly deserving. Let him wear a cap, let him toll the bells; he shall be our new court-fool: and, when the world is old and dead, the thin wit shall find the angel's record of man's works and deeds, and write with a lipless grin on the innocent first page for a title. "Here begins Death's Jest-book." (406)

The last line is a bit of self-conscious indulgence on Beddoes's part, yet ironically accurate; Isbrand's changing character and motives—from Jacobean revenger to aspiring hero and eventually egomaniac—will bring about the play's doomsday quality. Until now Isbrand thinks like the conventional jester and satirist ("if you would wound your foe, / Get swords that pierce the mind") even while plotting his revenge (419). But in the last third of the play his original motive is lost in a consuming ambition based not on some positive view of the world but rather on a repudiation of all its conventional values.

Nothing Either Above or Below

In act 1 Isbrand is essential only for purposes of the play's exposition; he does not become the central character until well into the second act. Initially he appears as a Jacobean revenge hero who, when his brother defaults on their mutual pledge to destroy their father's usurper, launches his own lonely campaign to achieve that end: "Isbrand, thou tragic fool, / Cheer up. Art thou alone? Why, so should be / Creators and destroyers" (343). But once the play has shifted from Ancona and Egypt to Germany, Isbrand gradually becomes more dominant and complex. By act 3 we are aware of the Jacobean malcontent in his character as well. The revenge hero and the malcontent are not always clearly distinct characters in Renaissance drama; frequently they share a skeptical, darkened vision of the world, a melancholy nature, and sometimes—certainly in the malcontent—a satirical perspective. These elements produce an ambiguity in both types, an ambiguity also recognizable in Hamlet. Isbrand possesses these qualities, particularly the ambiguous nature. And though like Conrad's Kurtz in *The Heart of Darkness* he transcends all moral restraint and becomes nearly inhuman in his negation, there is produced by that very act an emotional power and an authenticity that prevent simple moral censure;

we may disapprove of Isbrand but we cannot be unimpressed by him.

If Isbrand is, as Eleanor Wilner observes, "a kind of Hamlet without compunction,"[31] he yet retains his kinship with the tragic hero. But not only is that tragic hero more Jacobean than Shakespearean, he also emerges from a modification of literary tradition produced by Beddoes's own increasingly disordered vision. It is impossible fully to define Romantic tragedy, except by example—it is a dark, confused, murky world. But the line between tragic hero and Romantic villain is vague, and Beddoes's play fully participates in the ambiguity of a genre urged on by tradition and personal predilection, yet unable to find a firm base in common consent.

Romantic individualism could, in fact, only thrust out, and in so doing it risked clashing with social values; nor was there a deeper level of shared belief to be realized in mythic terms. The loss of a traditional sense of cosmic order—the sort of order that allows Shakespeare to return the world of Lear to normal at the play's conclusion—explains the frequently negative character of Romantic tragedy. While there is little apocalyptic optimism in Wordsworth's *The Borderers,* Byron's *Cain,* or Shelley's *The Cenci,* tragic anguish—but not the catharsis—remains from the traditional form. Hence, though all tragic heroes are isolated by the nature of their experience, Romantic heroes are still more cut off. Loneliness and isolation are the results of a more radical individualism, the enormous price to be paid for a Romantic ideal. Moreover, the desire for exclusive identity, which extreme individualism represents, is often paralleled by the longing for fusion with the absolute and hence complete impersonality—that other half of the Romantic paradox. Traditional tragedy resolves a similar paradox through the hero's eventual transcendence or reintegration, and that reintegration is possible because the higher order which the play finally affirms includes a social analogy, an example of which we see in *Lear.* But Romantic transcendence is a lonely and precarious business. Though deeply flawed, Oedipus and Macbeth come to represent for others the potential human greatness; Manfred, Beatrice Cenci, and Isbrand are never returned to the human norm. They learn only, as Wordsworth's Oswald declares in *The Borderers,* that "suffering is permanent, obscure and dark, / And shares the nature of infinity."[32] Isbrand is like Conrad's Kurtz in *The Heart of Darkness;* "there was nothing either above or below him. . . . He had kicked himself loose of the earth."

The Fool's Tragedy

The above discussion makes obvious that the play's interpretation demands a clear understanding of the ambiguous character of Isbrand. The jester has been viewed both as a successful aspiring hero and as Beddoes's portrait of an egomaniacal nihilist.

Agar sees the play as a "deterioration of a tragic hero's capabilities under stress of his mania," and points to Isbrand's cry of "Hate! Hate! Revenge and blood!" as an example of his limitation to a single passion.[33] Agar does not define "tragic"; however, the usual assumptions behind the term seem to suggest a contradiction. Tragic heroes do not generally deteriorate in the course of a drama; rather, they rise toward some moment of tragic dignity that redeems them and us. That Isbrand does not do so—or do so in the traditional way—suggests the confused and confusing tragic assumptions held by Beddoes and other Romantics.

When Beddoes has Isbrand declare his all-consuming commitment to revenge he is simply being faithful to the Elizabethan revenge tradition he admired and from which he borrowed basic materials when he wrote his play; Malevole in Marston's *The Malcontent* is clearly behind the jester, and the ghost of Wolfram has a long list of Renaissance ancestors. He was, moreover, capable of paying lip-service to the traditional theory of tragedy. "The pivot of all tragedy," he argues, is "the struggle between the will of man and the moral law of necessity" (651), a definition suitably broad enough to embrace both classical and Renaissance drama. But the play makes it quite clear that there is no real "moral law of necessity" at work in Beddoes's world, and the equation of Isbrand's nihilism with evil suggests the existence of a far more specific and conventionally Christian mythology than the play actually possesses. If the play is taken as evidence, Beddoes believes far more in will than in morality. Certainly this is a drama of will (without which, of course, it is difficult to conceive of any tragedy), and as a Romantic he had no difficulty asserting the dominance of that faculty in human affairs.

Tragedy, then, is for Beddoes a matter of mind, not morality. This attitude is evident in his conviction that the studies of dramatists and physicians are "closely, almost inseparably allied." Earlier, at least, he believed that science might assist art in the pursuit of truth. For example, the "science of psychology, & mental varieties, has long been used by physicians, in conjunction with the corresponding corporeal knowledge, for the investigation & removal of immaterial causes of disease; it still remains for some one to exhibit the sum of his experience in mental pathology & therapeutics, not in a cold technical dead description, but a living semiotical display, a series of anthropological experiments, developed for the purpose of ascertaining some important psychical principle—i.e., a tragedy" (609).

Here the new medical student perhaps intends to impress his friend Kelsall, but his reference to "mental pathology" is clear enough. To the end Beddoes's imagination would cleave to the great Renaissance drama he knew so well. But whatever the cultural trappings he retained from older drama, the necessity Beddoes posits in *Death's Jest Book* has little to do with traditional morality.

If Isbrand's character is the critical crux of the play, then two of his soliloquies, one concluding act 4 and the other ending the first scene of act 5, provide the key passages for any attempt to determine his nature. The first speech follows Siegfried's announcement of impending victory: loyalist forces "cannot stand another half hour." Left alone to savor his success, Isbrand indicates how far his motives have exceeded those of the revenge hero:

> O! it is nothing now to be a man.
> Adam, thy soul was happy that it wore
> The first, new, mortal members. . . .
> Thine was the hour to live in. Now we're common,
> And man is tired of being no more than human;
> And I'll be something better:—not by tearing
> This chrysalis of psyche ere its hour,
> Will I break through Elysium. There are sometimes,
> Even here, the means of being more than men:

And I by wine, and women, and the sceptre,
Will be, my own way, heavenly in my clay.
O you small star-mob, had I been one of you,
I would have seized the sky some moonless night,
And made myself the sun; whose morrow rising
Shall see me new-created by myself.
Come, come; to rest, my soul. I must sleep off
This old plebeian creature that I am.

(470)

Were his response to triumph to end here, we could accept these lines as simply metaphorical, an echo of Marlowe, perhaps. But after Siegfried has returned to inform him of the demands of his fellow conspirators and their expectations of a "new republic," Isbrand repudiates both democracy and, more importantly, his own human limitations:

A king's a man, and I will be no man
Unless I am a king. Why, where's the difference?
Throne steps divide us: they're soon climbed perhaps:
I have a bit of fiat in my soul,
And can myself create my little world.

(471–72)

The last line repeats the autonomy asserted near the end of the first soliloquy; even had he been born a dog, he claims, he would have "found the steps from dog to man, / And crept into his nature" (472). We are therefore prepared when, once more alone, Isbrand radically expands the scope of his first assertion:

                   How I despise
All you mere men of muscle! It was ever
My study to find out a way to godhead,
And on reflection soon I found that first
I was but half created; that a power
Was wanting in my soul to be its soul,
And this was mine to make. Therefore I fashioned
A will above my will, that plays upon it,
As the first soul doth use in men and cattle.
There's lifeless matter; add the power of shaping,
And you've the crystal: add again the organs,

Wherewith to subdue sustenance to the form
And manner of one's self, and you've the plant:
Add power of motion, senses, and so forth,
And you've all kind of beasts; suppose a pig:
To pig add foresight, reason, and such stuff,
Then you have man. What shall we add to man,
To bring him higher? I begin to think
That's a discovery I soon shall make.
Thus I, owing nought to books, but being read
In the odd nature of much fish and fowl,
And cabbages and beasts, have I raised myself,
By this comparative philosophy,
Above your shoulders, my sage gentlemen.
Have patience but a little, and keep still,
I'll find means, bye and bye, of flying higher.

(472)

Seigfried, even without hearing these last lines, declares to the others that Isbrand talks like one who has "made a bloody compact with some fiend" (473), but unlike Marlowe's Dr. Faustus and like Byron's Manfred, the jester has made no surrender to supernatural forces; this is his unaided concept of himself, the assertion of immense will.

The crucial soliloquy just quoted has been read as an indication of Beddoes's formulation of an evolutionary theory, as his combination of Kant's "absolute Will" and Ficthe's ego, as a version of Novalis's "Magic Idealism," as a forecast of Nietzsche, and as simply the final and overwhelming indication of Isbrand's mad overreach.[34] There is some truth in each of these arguments, with the probable exception of the first. But it is the last—Agar's—that comes closest to describing the reader's experience with the play. Agar's interpretation of Isbrand's character, however, is an indictment more than an analysis; it is impossible for the critic to recognize that Beddoes can create a character who will expose his own spiritual failure and still not design the play to be simply his repudiation.

Isbrand, it should be noted, attempts to retrieve a throne that, with the death of Wolfram, is quite literally his own. Melveric is the real usurper, having stolen the crown and destroyed its rightful owner. He has, moreover, killed the duke's heir and his own best friend. Melveric's evil is committed both before the play opens and again in the first act, and the development of Isbrand's character tends to obscure the duke's guilt. But these political facts, along with Mario's anachronistic appeal to liberty, remain largely beside the point; Isbrand's politics may begin in revenge but they end in the politics of despair. His subsequent desire for power is rooted in discontent, not malcontent; his overreach, like his satirical perspective, springs from the same confused but intense awareness of the disorder in the world, and hence his own terrible isolation.

To be isolated in Beddoes's world, to be cut off from humanity by actual conditions or by one's perception, often leads to a search for power. Leopold in *The Improvisatore,* for example, provides an early example. Marcello in the fragment *The Second Brother,* who shares qualities with both Melveric and Isbrand, returns home to seize his rightful throne and thrust himself into his younger brother's world not simply as a legitimate claimant but as a tyrant and an agent of almost cosmic revenge. In *Torrismond* it is the protagonist's despair and alienation that cause him to lament "the curse / Of being for a little world too great," and to demand "more than nature has to give" (271). Recognizing with Isbrand and Beddoes's other characters that for man the "mighty labor is to die," he swears that "we'll drive in a chariot to our graves, / Wheel'd with big thunder, o'er the heads of men" (283). The fragment ends with these lines, for Torrismond actually wishes to return to some preconscious state, like T. S. Eliot's "pair of ragged claws / Scuttling across the floors of silent seas":

>   unbeget me;
> For 'till I'm in thy veins and unbegun,
> Or to the food returned which made the blood
> That did make me, no possible lie can ever
> Unroot my feet of thee.
>   (283)

He can neither accept nor react to his father's repudiation; and his will to power, inevitably negative and backed by no real autonomy, results only in the strong lines previously quoted—spoken just before the fragment lapses into silence.

Driving over the heads of men is not an uncommon failing

in the tragic hero; indeed, it is part of the tragic paradox, as
Oedipus and Macbeth give witness. Isbrand, therefore, feeling
that he "was but half created," reverses Torrismond's desire
to be "unbegun" and projects a state above mankind. He would
thus remove himself from the enslavement of man's place in
the traditional hierarchical structure of all matter, life and spirit.
In so doing he also plays the part of the Romantic hero; Faust
and Manfred deny Pope's assertion of the neoclassical belief
that the great chain of being must be preserved.

However, *Death's Jest Book* evolves into "the fools tragedy"
and, as Frye reminds us, Isbrand loses the sense of irony that
would have preserved his awareness of moral fallibility.[35] Mandrake, who poses a truly comic and therefore healthy character,
argues at the play's opening that the fool "signifies humanity"
(329). Isbrand's attempt to finish his creation, to transcend his
human limitations through the unaided assertion of his own
Faustian will, defines the grounds of his role as radical satirist.
But seen from the tragic perspective, the same aspiration marks
his hubris. In this sense the critical lines on self-creation articulate
his pride at its most outrageous moment, and therefore occur
appropriately at the outset of the last act. Self-deceived almost
until the end, Isbrand can deny even his own death wound:
"I but pretend to die."

> I will live longer: when he's dead and buried,
> A hundred years hence, or, it may be, more,
> I shall return and take my dukedom back.
> Imagine not I'm weak enough to perish:
> The grave, and all its arts, I do defy.
>
> (484)

He can admit only in the last seconds of his life that he has
been death's, not life's, fool.

It is significant that there is no catharsis in Isbrand's fall, either
for Beddoes or the reader. The jester represents power wasted,
the will perverted. Beddoes's attempt to make a buffoon of
death becomes a tragedy of revenge; the tragedy of revenge
becomes the tragedy of man's hopeless conflict with absurdity.
Like Wordsworth's Marmaduke in *The Borderers,* Isbrand can
know only that "the world is poisoned at the heart."[36] For Bed-

does the admired genre retains its power only as a form for the expression of despair. "We who have little belief in heaven and still less faith in man's heart," he asks, "are we fit ministers for the temple of Melpome?" The question remains relevant. His own answer could be only "no—let Scandal & Satire be the only reptiles of the soul-abandoned corse [*sic*] of literature" (622). Whatever its Renaissance influences, then, the play becomes not a tragicomedy but a tragic satire, and the victim is as much Beddoes as it is the world. The poet, himself terribly self-isolated and admittedly antisocial, shared Isbrand's nihilism.

Beddoes as Mythopoeic Poet

In a note to his "Ode. Intimations of Immortality," concerned that his use of the Platonic concept of the preexistence of the soul might offend the religiously orthodox, Wordsworth pointed out that he had made the best possible use of the idea as a poet. This comment goes to the very heart of the Romantic enterprise. These poets had inherited a bankrupt spiritual and aesthetic orientation; one result of the Enlightenment had been the invalidation of the traditional myths that had made poetry possible in any comprehensive sense. While Blake's impressive attempt to create an imaginative order—"I must create a System or be enslaved by another Man's"[37]—is the most obvious example of the mythopoeic imagination vigorously at work in the period, all the Romantic poets sought, consciously or unconsciously, to provide themselves with some sort of cosmic syntax. Wallace Stevens in "Of Modern Poetry" gives a useful if late expression of the dilemma they faced; he defines "the poem of the mind in the art of finding / What will suffice. It has not always had / To find: the scene was set; it repeated what / Was in the script."[38]

Beddoes came to poetic maturity after the great rush of Romantic imaginative activity and creative optimism had passed. Wordsworth was well on his way to becoming Browning's "Lost Leader"; Coleridge had lapsed largely into talk; Shelley was dead, his major attempt—"The Triumph of Life"—left unfinished. Blake's more radical vision and the poetic structure it produced might have helped Beddoes, but by 1827 Blake, too, was dead and his work inaccessible. The Romantic sun had set. But even had it not, the modern act of poetic reconstruction is a private one; at best, other poets might provide encouragement, not working models. And perhaps even more important, Beddoes lacked the spiritual élan shared by the major Romantics in their most glowing moments; blighted early in some still not fully understood way, Beddoes was not equipped to take part in what might be called Romanticism's heroic phase.

Romantic myth was in large part energized by what is usually called the Romantic apocalyptic vision, and a visionary faith that evolved from an initial preoccupation with social change into a realization of individual spiritual potential. It is against this background that we must view Beddoes.

Like many, Wordsworth lamented the degenerate age he lived in, but with Coleridge and others of his generation he at first believed in the possibility of a categorical social change. Standing on the site of the recently demolished Bastille he picked up a stone and "pocketed the relic" of a holy war fought against ancient wrong, seeing in the French Revolution the opening chapter in the story of a renewed mankind. For Wordsworth and his contemporaries "Europe at that time was thrilled with joy, / France standing on the top of golden hours, / And human nature seeming born again."[39] When the revolution turned France into first a charnel house and later a hostile military camp, and when England repudiated the ideals of the revolution, Wordsworth entered a period of crucial change that led him from hope in the social apocalypse, through despair, to a belief in an inner, not outer, change. As M. H. Abrams puts it, "the hope has been shifted from the history of mankind to the mind of the single individual, from militant external action to an imaginative act."[40] From the internalization of apocalyptic idealism came the myth of the marriage of the mind of man and nature, and the new Eden it could produce. For Wordsworth as for Blake the barricades had come to be located in the mind and heart, not in the streets.

The case was different for Beddoes. As a young man he was deeply influenced by the example of Shelley, and he vigorously shared the liberal convictions of his generation. But neither did he come of age at the outset of the French Revolution as had the first generation of Romantics, nor was he temperamentally able to sustain the second generation's idealism. Moreover, the crushing victory of German absolutism over the liberal political movement in which he had taken an active part as a medical student reinforced his natural tendency and left him little room for any real optimism concerning social change. Lacking spiritual resiliency he, too, would internalize his own apocalyptic longings, but only in some negative way.

We have seen how Beddoes's deep pessimism emerges in *Death's Jest Book* as doomsday satire marked by a powerful sense of the absurdity and futility of life, a pessimism intensified by the failure of his scientific studies to find an alternative source of life-giving knowledge. Blake, too, resorts to apocalyptic satire—for example, in *The Marriage of Heaven and Hell*—yet despite his similar modernity the attack is essentially positive, for it is based, like traditional satire, on an idealistic view of man's potential for change. Beddoes's satire is, however, pervasively negative, because it originates in a profoundly modern sense of life's radical absurdity. Thus, while the myths of Blake and Wordsworth offer positive metaphors of rebirth and reintegration, Beddoes's imagination can linger only on dissolution and death.

And yet it would be wrong to conclude from this that Beddoes did not share the common Romantic impulse toward larger imaginative structure. As we have earlier seen, his very choice of genres implies such an impulse; the extended forms—and *Death's Jest Book* is almost epic in scope—offered the means to realize that impulse, if they did not actually demand it. As Herbert Lindenberger has pointed out, "the dramatic convention often provided an ideal outlet for an essentially lyric impulse which, not resting satisfied with the modest framework of the short poem, demanded a more comprehensive structure to express a larger vision."[41] But more important evidence lies in his compulsive and repetitive use of specific themes, situations, and characters—precisely those elements that define the mythopoeic urge in Wordsworth. Whereas Wordsworth is compelled to return again and again in his major poetry to images of the creative interchange of man and nature, Beddoes's imagination circles endlessly around the relationship between life and death. The result for Wordsworth is the myth of "the active universe" dramatized in such poems as "Michael" and *The Prelude*. Beddoes returns repeatedly to the universe of death in all his poetry and conclusively in *Death's Jest Book*.

A Solace for the World's Remorseless Harm: The Apotheosis of Death

What we have seen happen to Beddoes's *Death's Jest Book* during the course of composition and revision is the transformation of what might have been a typically eclectic and derivative Romantic drama into an extraordinary fusion of doomsday satire and what can be loosely termed existential tragedy. Isbrand has neither risen triumphant and terrible as a Jacobean revenger nor succeeded as a Faustian hero. He ends in self-defeat, having had—for all his Titanism—the capacity only to extend but not transcend Torrismond's negative will to power. Death, whatever its actual nature, has proven to be no vulnerable "dotard" after all, and Beddoes's promise to "conquer . . . and kill" the great dread ends in failure.

The Brides' Tragedy demonstrates Beddoes's preoccupation with the demon-lover theme and the way in which love leads increasingly to death for Hesperus and his brides: Eros becomes Thanatos. For Hesperus the problematical nature of his divided loyalties intensifies his passion, and passion leads him to seek and give death. That realization can be achieved only in death creates the play's tragic irony; as much as he seeks fulfillment in death he also seeks escape. The narrow scope of the play and its closer adherence to the Jacobean mode allows a dramatic closure that becomes impossible in the later work.

We have also noted Beddoes's ambivalent treatment of death in the earlier play; it is largely by refusing to face its full implications, or by distorting and muting those implications, that the play is successfully closed. Like Coleridge's *Ancient Mariner* the work is finished through some sleight of hand; in both authors' works the contradictory elements are ignored, not resolved. In the case of *Death's Jest Book* the proper analogy is with Coleridge's "Christabel." Coleridge could not proceed twice by fiat, and the poem remains unfinished, hedged about by deceptive explanations and rationalizations. *Death's Jest Book* grows larger during endless revision, and the problems of theme, which Beddoes is able partially to ignore in *The Brides' Tragedy,* create a permanent impasse in the later play. In a sense concluded but certainly never finished, the play remained Beddoes's constant burden—a perpetual reminder of his failure to clarify his imaginative vision. But the vision, in all its inconsistency, remained compelling to Beddoes, right down to the moment when he chose to translate imagination back into experience, poetry into final experiment. And that Beddoes's suicide shared the confused realization-escape dichotomy of the vision itself appears obvious.

Throughout Beddoes's poetry, death is seen in a curiously Germanic way; the death wish as found in German Romantic literature, but more rarely in English poetry with the partial exception of Keats, is constant in Beddoes. And despite Beddoes's self-avowed intentions, *Death's Jest Book* treats the condition of death with respect, sometimes with humor, and often with a kind of affectionate, if baffled, longing—however much dying may seem to be the ultimate joke. Human weakness, not death, is the butt of the jest.

This attitude is emphasized by fragments he composed for the play during the twenty or so years following its initial completion. Here, for example, is the way he later describes Wolfram's death:

> Aye, nobly doffed he his humanity.
> The bodily cloud that veiled his majesty
> Melted away into the elements
> As clouds from off a sunny mountain's pinnacle:
> 'Twas to die nobly.
>
> (493)

And noble to die because, as Isbrand says in another late passage, "Death is mightier, stronger, and more faithful / To man, than Life" (496).

Describing the death wish in Beddoes, Heath-Stubbs argues that sometimes "Death is seen as a state of mystical and transcendental union with the Universe."[42] There certainly are moments when—painfully aware of "man's frail and perilous tenure" on earth—Beddoes feels that to be "alone in the eternal is my hope" (491). Man can find

> comfort in the stars and flowers
> Apparelling the earth and evening sky,
> That moralize throughout their silent hours,

And woo us heaven-wards till we wish to die;
Oft hath he singled from the soothing quire,
For its calm influence, some of softest charm
To still his bosom's pangs, when they desire
A solace for the world's remorseless harm.

(489)

The world is life as we know it: the aging of our mixed
states, sure destruction, sense of the absurd. But what is the
heaven toward which lovely nature pulls us? These same stars,
however beautiful, however much they may provoke the perpetual search for signs of possible transcendence, actually "look
untouched down through the moony rain" on man, "ignorant,
not in scorn, of his affection's bent" (489). They remain enig-
matic and indifferent. Beddoes's ever-present flowers, on the
other hand, link man more nearly to nature herself, to the endless cycle of birth, decay and death, than to some eternal essence.
In Beddoes's poetry we are forever "turning to daisies gently
in the grave" (243), a realization that for Beddoes is devoid
of the usual Western grimness and terror.

Heath-Stubbs's description, on the whole, would appear to
better describe Wordsworth, Shelley, or even Whitman than
Beddoes, who seems to find some unspecified vague fusion with
material nature, rather than with a more spiritual aspect of the
cosmos. As Knight points out, in Beddoes's work "death speaks
through fecund nature, especially flowers."[43] Higgens adds that
death for Beddoes reflects no philosophical position; "it is purely
emotional."[44] The latter observation might seem curious on the
face of it, yet it is actually very apt. Neither in his scientific
empiricism nor in his poetic vision is Beddoes—any more than
other English Romantics and rather less than Shelley—a philosopher. At any rate, whether personified, dramatized, or seen as
a state of being, death for Beddoes is nearly always concrete,
and, despite his very different attitude, not totally unlike the
condition Robert Browning's materialistic cleric plans for himself in "The Bishop Orders his Tomb."

The character of Mandrake provides a comic treatment of
this state; believing himself dead he comes to recognize death
as a "fictitious condition," deliberately distorted to frighten off
the living: "after all being dead's not so uncomfortable when

one's got into the knack of it" (423). In a serious inversion
of Mandrake's delightfully absurd state, the genuinely dead Wolfram says to his brother,

> Excuse me. I am absent,
> And forget always that I'm just now living.
> But dead and living, which are which? A question
> Not easy to be solved. Are you alone,
> Men, as you're called, monopolists of life?
> Or is all being, living? and *what is,*
> With less of toil and trouble, more alive,
> Than they, who cannot, half a day, exist
> Without repairing their flesh mechanism?
> Or do you owe your life, not to this body,
> But to the sparks of spirit that fly off,
> Each instant disengaged and hurrying
> From little particles of flesh that die?
> If so, perhaps you are the dead yourselves:
> And these ridiculous figures on the wall
> Laugh, in their safe existence, at the prejudice,
> That you are anything like living beings.
>
> (482)

This speech illustrates the special paradox of Beddoes's poetic
fiction. In the awkward expression "repairing their flesh mecha-
nism" we hear the physician-scientist and, in "monopolists of
life," the artist who envisions death's painted dancers as potentially more "alive" and certainly more secure than the nominal
living—a sort of Beddoesian version of appearance and reality.
    Frye argues that Beddoes believes, "not that there is 'life
after' death, but that life and death are different aspects of the
same world," that man "is the seed of a ghost."[45] Such may
well be the case; clearly Beddoes offers a parallel existence:

> In the old times Death was a feverish sleep,
> In which men walked. The other world was cold
> And thinly-peopled, so life's emigrants
> Came back to mingle with the crowds of earth:
> But now great cities are transplanted thither,
> Memphis, and Babylon, and either Thebes,
> And Priam's towery town with its one beech.
> The dead are most and merriest: so be sure

> There will be no more haunting, till their towns
> Are full to the garret; then they'll shut their gates,
> To keep the living out, and perhaps leave
> A dead or two between both kingdoms.
>
> (434)

This witty yet serious speech by Siegfried illustrates the concrete nature of that other world, which we, with our "prejudice," dread and hence malign. In fact, Beddoes's world of death differs less from life in its order of reality than one would naturally assume; he is no mystic seeking the infinite but rather a poet peopling the landscape of his vision.

It should not be surprising, then, that however much Isbrand may bitterly resist death, its attractions are obvious to others. From the comic pleasure of Mandrake in his fictitious demise, to Wolfram's successful wooing of Sibylla in death, character after character looks to death—at least momentarily—for realization or release. Athulf attempts suicide, saying, "my soul shall cut itself a door / Out of this planet" (453); both Sibylla and Amala consider dying as their best hope; and, perhaps more remarkable, Duke Melveric first seeks his dead wife's resurrection and then later, when he has helped crush the rebellion against his throne, goes willingly and alive into that dark world with Wolfram, its gentle ambassador.

The Hieroglyphic Human Soul: The Moral World of *Death's Jest Book*

It is not by accident that of the main characters only Wolfram, killed early in the play, is unambiguously good. Despite his involvement in the Eros-Thanatos theme that links him to the murderous Hesperus in *The Brides' Tragedy*, Wolfram is no demon lover even if dead, and we can take him as Beddoes's spokesman on the subject of death's true nature. We have seen in Siegfried's speech a hint concerning death's positive character. Wolfram, who has better evidence, having had some experience in the matter, makes the point more directly in terms of the dead themselves:

> fear not me.
> The dead are ever good and innocent,

> And love the living. They are cheerful creatures,
> And quiet as the sunbeams, and most like,
> In grace and patient love and spotless beauty,
> The new-born of mankind.
>
> (452)

There is no irony intended here, although we are conditioned to expect it. However vaguely defined, death appears to be the superior state.

The superiority of death becomes clearer when we compare it with the living world in the play, a world marked by frequent inconsistencies between character and psychological norms, actions and moral values. Nearly all of Beddoes's critics note the instability of his characters, and most are content to attribute such instability to the author's failure as a dramatist.[46] But Beddoes is obviously an astute observer of other playwrights, and there is no reason to conclude that he is incapable of recognizing the psychological inconsistencies of his own creations. We have earlier suggested that his use of character is fundamentally different from that of other dramatists. However, at the symbolic level such inconsistency can actually be seen, from his perspective, as realism; the laws of human character trusted by other writers betray a desire to rationalize human nature. When Isbrand, already self-deluded by his increasing power, boasts of his profound understanding of the minds of the townspeople, Duke Melveric replies in a crucial speech:

> never hope to learn the alphabet,
> In which the hieroglyphic human soul
> More changeably is painted than the rainbow
> Upon the cloudy pages of a shower,
> Whose thunderous hinges a wild wind doth turn.
>
> (425)

The duke recognizes that "each doth shift his thought / More often in a minute, than the air / Dust on a summer path" (425–26).

In Melveric's analysis of human nature, one is reminded of Dostoyevsky in *Notes from Underground*. From his metaphoric hole in the floor the Underground Man ruthlessly exposes the common delusion of rational and consistent human behavior. Man is driven almost entirely by his will, he argues; it is choice,

whim, or fancy that dictates human action. The Underground
Man is a member of the psychological left; as such his radical
view of human nature assumes that the only consistency in human behavior is inconsistency, and that man's most obvious
quality is his perversity. Beddoes, too, sees man's essentially
irrational nature, and with that recognition comes—at the expense of his Enlightenment origins and liberal political faith—
a grim sense of the inescapably evil behavior such willfulness
must produce. Wilmer has made the point very succinctly; of
all the Romantics "only Beddoes seems to have had the deep
moral sense and the moral courage (and perhaps the masochism)
to see how the nature of things mocked morality; to see violence,
passion, and the abuse of power not as an aberration of human
life, but as somehow endemic to it. And he had the imagination
and insight to perceive that villains do not repent, that conscience
makes them not docile but more monstrous, that their self-hate
bodies them forth to their own imaginations as something inhuman and ugly, and that this ugliness becomes the law of their
beings."[47] Among the play's minor characters this condition is
well illustrated by Athulf's shifting response to his brother, cul-
minating in his murder of Adalmar. Among the major characters
Melveric, who so clearly recognizes man's hieroglyphic soul
and is a radical example of its willfulness, shifts his moral nature
several times during the play. Both Melveric and Athulf allude
to "Remorse," that cleansing if ambiguous state of mind ad-
vanced by several Romantic writers and experienced by Hesperus; both, however, pointedly reject it. Their responses are
similar; the duke, contemplating his own evil, asks, "who should
be merrier than a secret villain?" (422). Athulf, regretting his
own bad behavior but unable to avoid it, cries, "I was born
for sin and love it" (453).

In his gloomier moments Melveric sadly concludes that the
world has become "a hoary atheistic murderous star" (413)
and that "nothing's true / But what is horrible" (444). In this
vision he reflects Beddoes's own doomsday satire. But at other
moments he teaches his son that "Justice and Good / All penni-
less, base, earthly kind of fellows," are weak substitutes for
the pleasures of asserting a royal will (448). When a transient
love comes in conflict with his close relationship with Wolfram
he decides that "friendship, esteem, faith, hope, and sympathy,

/ We need no more" (361). There are times when his response to the rebellion in his dukedom, or to his son's familial disloyalty, appears as honorable as could be expected of any genuinely moral hero. But there is no permanent moral center in the duke, and subsequent action always undercuts the earlier impression of good.

In general, the moral world of the play is repeatedly marked by examples of the gap between behavior and the assumed code. Everywhere one finds the betrayal of good, and human nature is seen strong only in moments of destructive passion. Neither the duke nor Isbrand offers the reader a model of human worth, and they clearly dominate the work. Against the painful chaos they represent, Beddoes opposes death and love, the latter possible only in the world of the former. Since to die is to be "no more excepted from Eternity" (399), it comes as no surprise that the "spirit of retribution" acting through Wolfram does not kill Melveric. Rather, in the final moment of the play he imposes an appropriately Beddoesian revenge on the duke:

> Blessing and Peace to all who are departed!
> But thee, who daredst to call up into life,
> And the unholy world's forbidden sunlight,
> Out of his grave him who reposed softly,
> One of the ghosts doth summon, in like manner,
> Thee, still alive, into the world o' th' dead.
>
> (487)

Death's Jest Book, for all its unfinished quality, has the power to move its readers, but it could not express a saving vision for Beddoes where none existed. Already by 1828 "the truth was restless in him, / And shook his visionary fabrics down" (103). Born out of daring and desperate speculation, brooded over through years of increasing skepticism and despair, the work could be put aside only when Beddoes was himself no longer excepted from eternity.

Chapter Five

The Poet

Throughout his life Beddoes maintained his loyalty to the genre of Shakespeare and his fellow dramatists. Again and again he returned to *Death's Jest Book,* endlessly revising and enlarging it, and he eventually recast the entire first act—itself the length of many Greek tragedies. But the nondramatic poet as well remained alive in him and, relatively speaking, much of his creative output consisted of the lyric poetry written around (and for) the plays. When one removes the juvenilia and German translations from Donner's variorum edition, the reader is left with roughly ninety pages of nondramatic poetry, and many of these poems are versions of songs included in the plays. In that small collection one finds only a handful of remarkable poems. But, as George Saintsbury long ago asserted, with those few works Beddoes "attains to that small and disputed . . . class of poets who, including Sappho, Catullus, some mediaeval hymn-writers, and a few moderns, especially Coleridge, have, by virtue of fragments only, attained a higher position than many authors of large, substantive, and important poems."[1] Like the demanding Professor Saintsbury, other early modern critics considered Beddoes's lyrical poetry to justify fully his reputation, and they vigorously praised the author of such poems as "Dream-Pedlary" and "Song on the Water," believing that Beddoes "holds his patent far more on the strength of the songs and lyrics which he seems to have held in light esteem, than by the dramas at which he laboured so fiercely."[2]

Recent critics, however, attracted to the essentially modern quality of the great drama as well as to its intrinsic value, have come to prize *Death's Jest Book* above the lyrics, just as modern scholars have slowly come to realize the greater importance of Byron's *Don Juan* over his *Childe Harold.* Such a usually fine judge of poetry as Ian Jack has even gone so far as to argue that "as a lyric poet Beddoes is seldom at his best."[3]

However, Beddoes is *everywhere* a very uneven poet, and though the centrality of *Death's Jest Book* is essential to any modern appraisal, earlier critics, unimpressed by the significance of "modernity," were correct in their praise.

In most of his nondramatic poetry, even in those poems that have no connection with the plays, Beddoes is preoccupied with the expression, rather than exploration, of those themes with which he is always obsessed: life and death, the material and immaterial, Eros and Thanatos. Most combine Beddoes's unusual point of view and style with traditional lyrical elements. A smaller number, however, are more unique; in these poems appears the grotesque element so much a part of *Death's Jest Book.* A few poems fuse something of that grotesque quality with the lyric mode to produce works that epitomize his peculiar imagination. But before we discuss specific examples of these categories it will be useful to locate Beddoes in the poetic landscape of early-nineteenth-century English poetry, and also to describe his own attitude toward himself as a poet.

The "Owl-Season" of Contemporary Poetry

Beddoes wrote at the end of a period of enormous creativity, one that inevitably cast a long and intimidating shadow over many subsequent writers. He was, in addition, isolated by temperament and geography from his contemporaries. More important, he possessed only an inverted or negative version of the primary Romantic vision. For these reasons all his poems, but especially his lyric works, suggest not the shared power and creative momentum of a rich age . . . but rather a retrospective and elegiac reflection of that period.

In 1824 it seemed to the unhappy Beddoes that the tragic "disappearance of Shelley from the world" had deprived his age of its spiritual sun, and the "tropical setting of that luminary" had left an "instant darkness and owl-season" (589). Shortly thereafter he lamented the failure of all "young verse-grinders" to follow his own example and "give way to the really inspired" (637). But who were the inspired and truly worthy descendants of the great Romantics? Almost totally isolated from England, by 1844 Beddoes was unaware of "one single fellow, who has the least nose for poetry, that writes" (677).[4] He could still

prophesy that, "amid the lyrical chirpings of . . . young English
sparrows, shall come an eagle, and fetch fire from the altar
Miltonic to relight the dark lanterns of Diogenes and Guy
Fawkes" (677). But this doctrinaire Romantic identification of
the spirit of Milton with the purging fire of the moral imagination could not prevent him from recognizing that in his age
"few are called . . . and none are [*sic*] chosen" (677).

Beddoes's letters here make clear his sense of the barren
and transitional character of poetry in his time. Convinced of
his own inadequacy he looked in vain for English (and German)
writers who might continue the second Renaissance. In the fragmentary "Stanzas Written in Switzerland" he asserts that one
"who lonely strays in England's oaky forest / Meets silence
drear," the Romantic "Aeolian breathings" having ceased:

> Where are the masters of the magic word,
>   Who reallumed the Promethean blaze
> And let old Ocean out with all his herd
>   On the Atlantic sufferer's front to gaze?
> Where he, whose satire sharper than sharp sword
>   Flashed and fell deep, unparried by amaze?
> Where he, of heath and lake most love of all
> In lady's bower and castled tower and hall
> With fairy-footed, dancing thoughts and longings musical?
>
> (155)

That Beddoes would lament the passing of Shelley and Keats
is not surprising; more interesting is the approval shown to
Byron, whom he had always disliked but who, when contrasted
with modern writers, shines with greatness.

Beddoes's "Lines Written in Switzerland" (intended as a prologue to a never-written poem on Prometheus) explores the
same ground as "Stanzas Written in Switzerland" and stands
as a sort of elegy for the Romantic movement—possibly even
the integrity of English letters. The poem's strength can be
attributed to his deep love for English poetry and concern for
its fate. It opens with the same pastoral reference to the "silence
drear in England's oaky forest" and goes on to lament especially
the loss of his chief English mentor, Shelley, and the associated
Keats:

> We, who marked how fell
> Young Adonais, sick of vain endeavour
> Larklike to live on high in tower of song;
> And looked still deeper thro' each other's eyes
> At every flash of Shelley's dazzling spirit,
> Quivering like dagger on the breast of night,
> That seemed some hidden natural light reflected
> Upon time's scythe, a moment and away:
> Darkness unfathomable over it.
>
> (156)

This is the same imagery with which Beddoes had captured Shelley's essence years before in the admirable "Lines Written in a Blank Leaf of the 'Prometheus Unbound.'" There Shelley is a "Spirit of the sun, / An Intellect ablaze with heavenly thoughts" who "sunned the dim world," a "flooding summer burst on Poetry" (67). To Beddoes Shelley epitomized the Romantic fire and light that had been lost beyond recall.

That such fire is associated in the later poem not only with poetic felicity but also with the democratic vision is clear in Beddoes's reference to "Mount Rydal's snowy head / Bound round with courtly jingles" (156). Rydal Mount was the home of the established and increasingly conservative William Wordsworth. Although Wordsworth was once thought of by such liberal writers as William Hazlitt as the French Revolution in English poetry, Beddoes implies that Wordsworth's true voice has been stilled, his silence purchased by royal gold.

Written late in his life, "Lines" shows the influence of Beddoes's long years of political activity and liberal thought. It may be excessive to argue, as Geoffrey Wagner has done, that Beddoes "loathed capitalism, which he equated especially with England";[5] as a foreigner amidst the political turmoil of Germany and Switzerland he had always prized his origins in democratic England. But Wagner is correct in labeling this poem Beddoes's "most splenic attack" on the country of his birth:

> Well, Britain; let the fiery Frenchman boast
> That at the bidding of the charmer moves
> Their nation's heart, as ocean 'neath the moon
> Silvered and soothed. Be proud of Manchester,
> Pestiferous Liverpool, Ocean-Avernus,

> Where bullying blasphemy, like a slimy lie,
> Creeps to the highest church's pinnacle,
> And glistening infects the light of heaven.
> O flattering likeness on a copper coin!
> Sit still upon your slave-raised cotton ball,
> With upright toasting fork and toothless cat:
> The country clown still holds her for a lion.
>   (156–57)

The target of the attack, however, is not the British economic system itself so much as it is the Philistine character of laissez-faire capitalism, the same quality that Matthew Arnold made such a heroic attempt to improve. The poem suggests that for the moment Beddoes is tempted to return to the battle himself— "once more [to] weave the web of thoughtful verse"—and presumably the intended poem on Prometheus would have continued the Romantic apocalyptic tradition. It is "Truth" (cited three times in ten lines) achieved through "genius" that he demands, and faithful to his own epistemological dualism he invokes both "Shakespeare, our recording angel," and "Newton, whose thought rebuilt the universe, / and Galileo, broken hearted seer, / Who, like a moon attracted naturally, / Kept circling round the central sun of Truth" (157).

"Lines Written in Switzerland" is a moving outburst, but the necessary energy and sense of direction cannot be maintained. The prologue slips away unfinished into a reminiscence of the Shelleyan world, and the poem on Prometheus—patron saint of Romantic revolt—never got written. His personal failure reinforces and merges with his sense of the lost generation here; English poetry will have to await another champion. Removed from English literary life and language, almost completely cut off now from his few remaining friends of the past, Beddoes was unaware of the great Victorian poets who were even then emerging out of that strange twilight world of later Romanticism.[6]

The Failure of Poetic Nerve

If Beddoes saw no sign of hope for poetry in the world around him, neither could he, finally, completely break "out of the

Alpine shade" (157) of his long self-exile or the creative paraly-sis he had come to feel. He considered himself to be "no writer for the time & generation" or even for posterity (639). We have earlier seen his deep-seated skepticism concerning his own creative talent, and the willingness with which he had embraced science as an alternative to literary effort. Donner has suggested that, as Beddoes's Continental years proceeded, the poet came to recognize his own poetic skill and gradually gained artistic self-confidence. The firmness of control in some individual poems suggests that such may have been the case, yet poems like "Lines Written in Switzerland" and his letters—always pain-fully honest and written as much perhaps to himself as to Kelsall and Procter—suggest otherwise. Once committed to Germany and the study of medicine he reevaluated his talent at length and concluded: "I am essentially unpoetical in character, habits & ways of thinking; and nothing but the desperate hunger for distinction, so common to young gentlemen at the Univy, ever set me upon rhyming" (636). His depression was deepened by the conviction that even men of such clearly "higher original-ity and incomparably superior poetical feeling and Genius" as Coleridge and Wordsworth "had done so little" (636).

In terms of the Romantic sensibility there existed another impediment to Beddoes's realization as a poet. He had chosen the drama as the most objective of genres, however ironic the actual result may have been. Subjectivity was, of course, the result of Romantic experience, not its program; both Coleridge, in his desperate attempt to make the painfully private "Dejec-tion: An Ode" more universal, and Wordsworth's concern for the nakedly autobiographical nature of *The Prelude,* illustrate the Romantic struggle against solipsism.

But the emergence of the private sensibility is inescapably at the heart of modern art, sometimes in joy but often in anguish. Beddoes's painful reticence is everywhere apparent, however; for instance, one has only to compare his letters, impressive as they are for their insight and judgment, with those of Byron or Leigh Hunt, to realize the iron privacy he retained. Beddoes absolutely rejected the art of "psychological self portraiture, fearing . . . to be betrayed into affectation, dissimulation, or some other alluring shape of lying." He believed that "all autobi-ographical sketches are the result of mere vanity—not excepting

those of St. Augustin & Rousseau" (664). That the argument
may be true—Dostoyevsky's Underground Man makes the same
complaint—is beside the point. Beddoes did not so far come
to understand himself and his age as to see that for modern
art, or much of it, the grounds of truth were inescapably subjective, even if the resultant poetry was not overtly autobiographical, that the nature of the modern experience would have to
be private first and public second, that subjectivity would at
times be its salvation. In fact, all Beddoes's best poetry, lyric
and dramatic, demonstrates that such is the case. But in Beddoes's work one detects self-conflict and resistance, a tension
that is only occasionally fruitful, and one that often chokes off
or at least subdues the experiential flow allowed to run its course
in the work of his great contemporaries. It is no doubt Beddoes's
intense reticence that accounts for the element of Romantic
irony that emerges in *Death's Jest Book* and derives not simply
from his great admiration for the German poet Ludwig Tieck
but also from an inner, instinctive need to protect himself.[7]

There are, however, moments when his poetry approaches
the Romantic confessional mode. In March 1828, for example,
Beddoes wrote a poem reminiscent of Coleridge's "Dejection:
An Ode." The seventy-nine-line "Written in an Album at Clifton" (a long poem for Beddoes) pretends to be telling the
story of an "almost unknown traveller" who when requested
writes a short passage in the poetry album of a very kind lady,
a passage describing his own blighted soul. Beddoes is, of course,
the traveler and he speaks of himself in the third person; the
lady is his beloved cousin Zoe King. He opens the poem with
an admission that the "lights and shadows of reality" had destroyed the inhabitants of his own creative universe, making
poetry nearly impossible. Likewise the "world-wandering
stranger" is unable to compose a story for the lady's album
and instead "left the way of fiction" to write of his own spiritual
bankruptcy and poetic failure. What Beddoes says of the stranger
is meant to apply to himself: "the truth was restless in him, /
And shook his visionary fabrics down" (103). Beddoes's poem
is clearly a parable of the failure of the poetry he esteems;
"visionary fabrics" equates with Romantic imaginative idealism.
The apocalyptic vision of, say, Shelley has been destroyed by
those "lights and shadows of reality." The poem thus provides

an indirect comment on Beddoes's state of mind: despair moderated by acceptance. Like Coleridge he had felt his "genial spirits fail"; the result was—again we think of Coleridge—the failure of both love and poetry.

Just as Beddoes speculated on the nature of drama and his own limitations in that genre, so, though to a much lesser degree, he considered lyric poetry. In 1829, perhaps with even more self-flagellation than usual as a result of Procter's criticism of the first version of *Death's Jest Book,* Beddoes denies his lyrical talent:

I have no real poetical call. I wd write more songs if I could, but I can't manage rhyme well or easily; I very seldom get a glimpse of the right sort of idea in the right light for a song—and eleven out of the dozen are always good for nothing. If I could rhyme well and order complicated verse harmoniously, I would try odes; but it's too difficult. (642–43)

One can only wish that Beddoes had attempted the Romantic ode. For Coleridge, Wordsworth, and especially Keats, the odal form, organically adapted to each poet's particular genius and perspective, had served to liberate intensely personal feelings and yet, disciplined by a lingering public quality traditionally inherent in the genre, to communicate a universal experience. And in addition to the Romantic ode's capacity for such mediation, it also offered a scope for poetic development neither as restricted as the brief lyric nor as demanding as the larger narrative or philosophical genres which required considerable organizational powers and, more significantly, a fully realized vision.

In 1830, predicting that he would "never be anything above a very moderate dabbler in many waters," Beddoes nevertheless maintained that he understood "song writing; it is almost the only kind of poetry of w^h I have attained a decided and clear critical theory." But he had also come to realize how difficult it was "to write a song with ease, tenderness, and that ethereal grace" that one finds in such writers as Shakespeare, Herrick, and Suckling (648, 649). But even if, as he argued, "eleven out of a dozen are always good for nothing," there remains the remarkable twelfth—the poem in which concept, diction, rhyme, prosody, and tone combine to create a lyric impact of

considerable, if subtle, power, a work that justifies Browning's
assertion that Beddoes was "the author of some of the finest
poetry of our time."[8] Such praise would have surprised Beddoes;
it is part of his tragedy that he did not live to hear it. A quatrain
tucked away in one of his manuscripts reveals both his longing
and his sense of failure:

> POOR bird, that cannot ever
>   Dwell high in tower of song:
> Whose heart-breaking endeavour
>   But palls the lazy throng.
>   (160)

The Tower of Song

Beddoes's longing for the "tower of song" frequently overcame his creative reticence, however. Just how many nondramatic poems Beddoes actually composed we can never know;
evidence points to his destruction of many works that may have
been too painful, or seemed to him clearly inferior. In fact,
like all of his work his nondramatic poetry is quite uneven.
We frequently encounter both the clichés of popular romanticism (with its overworked melancholy, residual Gothic elements,
and conventional nature and love imagery) and the habitual
gestures of Beddoes's own vocabulary of death. Early in his
career he often employed a derivative late-eighteenth-century
diction and personification that Wordsworth had promised to
eschew; at any point he may lapse into an enameled, artificial
literary language reminiscent of the early Keats and Leigh Hunt
or, more rarely, he may adopt the airy, speculative language
of Shelley. Some awareness of these less attractive qualities is
implied in Beddoes's self-satirical subtitle to the never-published
collection of poems he called "Outidana": "Effusions, Amorous,
Pathetic, and Fantastical."

There remains the largely successful group of poems that
has always caught the eye of certain critics from the nineteenth
century to the present. A few of these poems offer the reader
a more generalized experience—one demanding less knowledge
of or at least sympathy with his own peculiar point of view.

Among these are "Pygmalion: the Cyprian Statuary" and "To B. W. Procter, Esq.," both of which remind us that, however much he revered Shelley, Beddoes also knew his Keats.[9]

In the spring of 1825 Beddoes composed "Pygmalion" and with its completion never again returned to the middle-length narrative poem. Just two years before he had written the 346-line "Romance of the Lily"—very much in the style of *The Improvisatore* pieces discussed in an earlier chapter. Lacking causal logic or meaningful characterization, the earlier narrative serves only to remind us how badly a good poet may write. "Pygmalion," however, is rich in significance and resonant in language. Unlike the earlier poem its fully coherent theme results from Beddoes's deepest convictions rather than from the influence of popular literature.

"Pygmalion" tells the familiar story of the Greek sculptor who falls in love with his own creation—a lovely young woman—and whose genius is so great that he is able to give her life. Beddoes's Pygmalion finds a large stone of special quality and begins without hesitation to shape it into the form of his ideal; at the statue's completion he is immediately enthralled by her beauty. Unlike the original myth in which the artist is granted life for his creation and marriage to her as well, Beddoes causes his artist to die of grief at the very moment the statue quickens with life, convinced that he will never achieve the union of life and beauty. Beddoes is not, in other words, simply indulging in a perfunctory exploitation of a well-known myth, but rather seizing upon the symbolism, which in some ways seems most relevant to his own situation: the artist compelled to create but destroyed by that very creation.

Here is the poem's central paradox; Pygmalion is described as divine, an artist "who made the gods who made men" (78). Though human he is yet a "dealer of immortality / Greater than Jove himself" (81). As he does with Shelley, Beddoes associates Pygmalion's creative force with light: the moon first and then "bright and lonely as the sun / Like which he could create" (79). Once the great stone is safe in his studio he works incessantly, slipping out only at noon for air and sunshine, "till the life / Was too abundant in him and so rife / With light creative he went in alone / And poured it warm upon the

growing stone" (80). Yet for all his divinity he can never enjoy
the fruit of his creation—able to grant life he cannot participate
in the life he creates.

These last, lovely lines remind us of Keats, as does the poem's
opening passage:

> THERE stood a city along Cyprus' side
> Lavish of palaces, an arched tide
> Of unrolled rocks; and where the deities dwelled
> Their clustered domes pushed up the noon and swelled
> With the emotion of the god within,
> As doth earth's hemisphere, when showers begin
> To tickle the still spirit at its core
> Till pastures tremble and the river-shore
> Squeezes out buds at every dewy pore.
>
> (78)

But more than the style in "Pygmalion" is Keatsian; the subject,
too, suggests a common theme. Keats had continually made
the creation of art the subject of his poetry. His great odes
consist of a running debate on the nature of the imagination
and the reality that imagination reveals: "Was it a vision, or a
waking dream?" Eventually that question led to an answer frequently dramatized; imagination must be humanized—brought
to bear on the world of process—and the waking dream come
to be seen as a spurious reality dangerous to its possessor. Keats's
Lamia dramatizes just such a conclusion; the lovely Lamia de-
stroys Lycius (without wishing to) because he forces her to marry
him—reality and the waking dream cannot be joined.

Keats and Beddoes differ just here. Like Lamia, who, allegori-
cally speaking, is the product of Lycius's imagination, the marble
maiden is Pygmalion's own creation. But unlike Keats's Lamia
she is not illusory; she belongs to the immaterial world the
sculptor can evoke but not enter. Hence the beautiful lines
which show us her "cheek . . . growing human / With the
flushed distance of a rising thought / That still crept nearer"
also describe Pygmalion's parallel decline until "his foot is
stretching into Charon's barge" (82–83). In death "Elysium's
light illumines all his face," but the presence of "the sweet
woman-statue, quietly / Weeping the tears of his felicity" (83)
indicates the sentiment of the poem.

Douglas Bush, referring to the poem as Beddoes's *Alastor* or *Endymion,* suggests that Pygmalion "is a type of the lonely artist, the artist of an age of idealism, frustration, and *Weltschmerz,* whose life is apart from the world about him."[10] Donner argues that "so entirely has he given himself in the creation of the work of art that henceforward he is able to live only in the world of ideas, and to the life of this world he is dead for ever."[11] While both suggestions help us move beyond the surface of the poem toward an understanding of Beddoes's faith in the immaterial world, another compatible conclusion may be drawn. Pygmalion's creation is both a voluntary action and a leading from above; we are told that "he carved it not" since "the winged tool as digging out a spell / Followed a magnet" (81). When the poet asks, "What art thou now, divine Pygmalion?" and adds "thou hast done / That glory which hast undone thee for ever" (81), he emphasizes the poem's painful irony; if art is the full realization of the self, it may also displace the self and, symbolically, destroy it. Pygmalion's creation is actually Beddoes's "Belle Dame sans merci"; her willingness to reciprocate Pygmalion's love does not change her destructive nature, which, ironically, is the result of the modern artist's narcissistic nature. The poem never lets us forget that "the loved image stepping from his breast . . . therefore loves he it" (81). In this sense the poem is clearly a parable of the Romantic artist's potentially dangerous conflation of self and art.

"Pygmalion" is hardly "colourless, a literary gesture," as Snow would have us believe, either in language or in theme.[12] It is, however, very different from Beddoes's verse letter "To B. W. Procter, Esq.," whose subtitle, "From Oxford; May, 1825," indicates that it may have been written as little as a month after the narrative poem. It offers both a more private and, at the same time, more public poem. As a verse epistle it responds directly to his own situation; these eighty-five lines are ostensibly written to lure his friend Procter from that "smoky-faced Augustan town" (86) to spring-blessed Oxford. But the focus here is not in the least on Beddoes himself; rather he tries to evoke a delightful world for its own sake, and the appeal to Procter is merely an excuse for the attempt. Thus the private poem is actually more impersonal and objective than the story drawn from myth.

The epistle opens on a note of pleasant excitement; Beddoes is alert to the resurgence of nature as it prods intellectual Oxford into life. One may be reminded of Gerard Manley Hopkins's "Duns Scotus's Oxford," especially in the second line:

> IN every tower that Oxford has is swung,
> Quick, loud, or solemn, the monotonous tongue
> Which speaks Time's language, the universal one
> After the countenance of moon or sun,
> Translating their still motions to the earth,
> I cannot read; the reeling belfry's mirth
> Troubles my senses; therefore, Greek, shut up
> Your dazzling pages.
>
> (84)

But there are stronger associations with Wordsworth and the debate between natural piety and abstract learning in his "Expostulation and Reply" and "The Tables Turned." As with the persona of those two poems, what calls Beddoes here is "that which is not read, / Nor wrung by reasoning from a resolute head; / But comes like lightning on a hill-top steeple; / Heaven's spillings on the lofty laurelled people" (84). The usual Romantic attitudes are thus quickly established; nature's ally is imagination, not reason. Beddoes is quite willing to fold the "fat square blossoms" of learning's plant and introduce Procter to Oxford's real joys:

>   Here thou at morn shalt see
> Spring's dryad-wakening whisper call the tree
> And move it to green answers; and beneath,
> Each side the river which the fishes breathe,
> Daisies and grass whose tops were never stirred,
> Or dews made tremulous, but by foot of bird.
> And you shall mark in spring's heaven-tapestried room
> Yesterday's knoppe burst by its wild perfume,
> Like woman's childhood, to this morning's bloom;
> And here a primrose pale beneath a tree,
> And here a cowslip longing for its bee,
> And violets and lilies every one
> Grazing in the great pasture of the sun
> Beam after beam, visibly, as the grass
> Is swallowed by the lazy cows that pass.
>
> (85)

After Beddoes has offered Procter the bribe of an Oxford spring, he threatens him with a series of mock curses to be imposed on his friend should he reject his invitation. The poem closes with these witty possibilities and there are, for once, no sad reverberations to linger in the reader's mind. What is striking here is not Beddoes's reverence for nature—throughout his life he remained open to her "green answers"—but rather the note of unreserved gaiety and sense of celebration. The tone is playful, light, vivacious. The whimsical quality will be found again in the odd mixture of horror and humor that marks such very Beddoesian lyrics as "The Phantom-Wooer," but never again with such normal, healthy pleasure.

"Through Robe and Rib": Death's Own Poet

Typically Beddoes's nondramatic poetry—again and again directed, like the plays, toward death—is neither as intellectually nor as psychologically accessible as are the two poems we have just discussed. From the juvenilia, with their derivative Gothicism, to the late fragments bearing Beddoes's unique stamp, piece after piece is given over to the same grim obsession. Any number of lyrics and songs include the vocabulary of death in their title (for example, "The Ghosts' Moonshine," "Threnody," "Dirge"), but other works may open innocently enough before shifting, at least by the poem's end, to the old preoccupation. We have examined the theme in some detail in previous chapters, but it will be useful to sketch in its outline here.

As a child Beddoes was exposed to death in a most direct way. As the son of an experimental physician and a man who apparently felt that exposure to mortal reality would shape the boy's mind in a constructive way, Beddoes saw at first hand the physical husk that had late housed a glowing life. Perhaps the childhood experience with dissections had something to do with the development of his taste in literature. At any rate popular fiction and poetry on the subject certainly cooperated with his own inclination and experience, and help explain his fascination with the paradoxes of life and death.

His mother's death in Italy when he was twenty-one years old may have moved him from an intellectual and aesthetic interest in the subject toward a more deeply felt need to under-

stand what death meant; from that point on he seems to have
grown in his determination to explore the mystery. Hence a
young man with a promising career in the world of letters seized
upon medicine as a profession, and his long stay on the Continent
consists of an extended attempt to reach through science the
meaning of death and its relationship to life, while simultaneously allowing his imagination to range over the same ground
and produce his peculiar poetry.

We have earlier seen that the nature and significance of death
never became clear to Beddoes—despite his continual exploration of the subject in his art and the pursuit of it in his medical
studies. With the failure of both imagination and reason to answer the great questions, Beddoes's despair deepened and his
somber resignation grew. However, Beddoes never surrendered
the hope that the finite, material world would give way to the
infinite, spiritual world, and his unhappiness in the former caused
him to seek happiness in the latter. For that reason, in his poetry,
Beddoes frequently reverses the nature and value of life and
death, and in so doing portrays death and the world beyond
in remarkable ways. We have seen this to be the case in his
extraordinary *Death's Jest Book,* though in that work the break-
down of creative logic leaves Beddoes—and the reader—unsure
of its significance in the very work intended to resolve the issue.
In his nondramatic poetry, however, Beddoes feels himself to
be under no obligation to achieve a mythic or metaphysical
resolution; this poetry explores the strange land between the
states of life and death without attempting to produce an accurate
and detailed map of the region.

A good introduction to this strange landscape is his "Lines
Written at Geneva; July 16 [1824]," an unfinished poem that
nonetheless reminds us of its principal features. This meditative
poem opens with a contemplation of the night sky over the
lake, makes mention of the dead who have made for themselves
"blue pillows on Geneva's sea," and goes on to speculate on
the death of sound, suggesting that an "echo, is its ghost" (74).
Considering the dead in general, the poet argues that those
longest gone "who have seen their bodies moulder away" are
the happiest, since they "have no body but the beauteous air,
/ No body but their minds" (74). Others, "lying with the last
and only bone / Of their old selves," are forced to contemplate

the worm "that ate their hearts" (74); still others more newly dead—"their weary flesh, like an unused mansion, sold / Unto a stranger"—stand aside and "see enter it / The earthquake winds and waters of the pit, / Or children's spirits in its holes to play" (74). These images remind us of his preoccupation with the *physical* "reality" of dying, which in an earlier fragment he could relish:

> Then, if the body felt, what were its sense,
> Turning to daisies gently in the grave,
> If not the soul's most delicate delight
> When it does filtrate, through the pores of thought,
> In love and the enamelled flowers of song?
>
> (243)

Here, however, we see the poet's ambivalence toward the body, which, as anatomist and dissector, he knew so well. Donner has spoken of the "terror" in "Lines,"[13] and certainly we can catch a certain Shelleyan longing for essence and escape from the vulnerable flesh. But the final lines suggest an odd humor, too; Beddoes enjoys the last image of the children playing in the unused mansion of the body, a possibility he imagines on a very literal level. At any rate, both as physician and poet he had long believed that "through robe and rib and muscle to heart's core / We see as stars through clear midnight" (158).

But Beddoes can, on occasion, treat the subject of death's meaning more abstractly. The almost epigrammatic "Dirge," for instance, succinctly states one often-articulated position. This is the whole poem:

> TO-DAY is a thought, a fear is to-morrow,
> And yesterday is our sin and our sorrow;
> And life is a death,
> Where the body's the tomb,
> And the pale sweet breath
> Is buried alive in its hideous gloom.
> Then waste no tear,
> For we are the dead; the living are here,
> In the stealing earth, and the heavy bier.
> Death lives but an instant, and is but a sigh,
> And his son is unnamed immortality,

Whose being is thine. Dear ghost, so to die
Is to live—and life is a worthless lie.
Then we weep for ourselves and wish thee good-bye.
                                                                            (75)

Here physical life is almost a disgrace, almost a sin against the
ideal state. Or, if not a kind of failure, life is at least a condition
to escape, as the following early fragment maintains:

Is it not sweet to die? for, what is death,
But sighing that we ne'er may sigh again,
Getting a length beyond our tedious selves;
But trampling the last tear from poisonous sorrow,
Spilling our woes, crushing our frozen hopes,
And passing like an incense out of man?
                                                                            (243)

That such an escape, Beddoes usually implies, is toward, not
away from, something, that the real motivation is the achieve-
ment of immortality, not the escape from earthly pain, cannot
change the sadness of mortal life.

Perhaps his loveliest lyric—the delicate and wistful "Dream-
Pedlary"—focuses on the failure of imagination to make this
world acceptable. The first stanza establishes both the poignant
tone and the situation:

IF there were dreams to sell,
    What would you buy?
Some cost a passing bell;
    Some a light sigh,
That shakes from Life's fresh crown
Only a roseleaf down.
If there were dreams to sell,
Merry and sad to tell,
And the crier rung the bell,
    What would you buy?
                                                                            (110)

The ancient cry of the street pedlar becomes that of the dream
seller. The answer to his question given in stanza 2 is "a cottage
lone and still," a retreat to soothe his woes until death. The

third stanza brings disapproval of that choice: "ill dids't thou buy; / Life is a dream, they tell, / Waking, to die" (110). Rather than buy the dream of escape into isolation, the speaker suggests a "dream to prize," the ability to raise ghosts. Given that choice, the fourth stanza attempts to identify the ghost to raise—"my loved longlost boy"—but concludes that "vain is the call" (111). The final stanza completes this sad meditation:

> Know'st thou not ghosts to sue?
> No love thou hast.
> Else lie, as I will do,
> And breathe thy last.
> So out of Life's fresh crown
> Fall like a rose-leaf down.
> Thus are the ghosts to woo;
> Thus are all dreams made true,
> Ever to last!
>
> (111)

The final lines reverberate with pathos; "if" has been the poem's key word (opening stanzas 1 and 4), and Donner's conclusion that the poem conveys the "tragedy of an impossibility" seems correct.[14]

"Dream-Pedlary" has been much admired, especially for its delicate and intricate prosody.[15] Beddoes here, as in few other poems, is the absolute master of rhyme and meter. His deft manipulation of sound no doubt accounts for much of the poem's subtlety. But critics have not commented on another source of complexity in such an apparently simple work. Their appreciation usually focuses on the lovely first stanza and ignores the poem's sequence of question and answer, which actually constitutes a kind of internal dialogue. These exchanges, clear enough in stanzas 1 and 2, become more compressed in the last three stanzas; for instance one cannot be absolutely sure which voice is speaking in the first lines of stanza 3.

This somewhat elliptical quality adds to the poem's mystery without limiting its effectiveness. The burden of the last stanza is, after all, clear; love is essential if one is to make contact with the permanent world of the dead: "know'st thou not ghosts

to sue? / No love thou hast" (111). It is only through love
that "all dreams [are] made true" (111), and the sadness here
is, as Snow puts it, that of "the living who yearn for the dead,
rather than that of the dead yearning toward life."[16]

"Dirge and Hymeneal": The Thanatos-Eros Theme

As we have seen in the plays and again in "Dream-Pedlary,"
death and love are intimately connected in Beddoes's poetry.[17]
Although Romantic literature, especially German, frequently
makes this identification, it is the single most important theme
in Beddoes's nondramatic poetry. Beddoes makes no attempt
in these poems to analyze the identification; he simply asserts
it and allows the implications to form. In "Athulf's Song," from
Death's Jest Book, we are offered "a cypress-bough, and a rose-
wreath sweet, / A wedding-robe, and a winding sheet, / A
bridal-bed and a bier," for "Death and Hymen both are here"
(100). In "Dirge and Hymeneal" Beddoes's own headnote describes the context in which takes place the duet that follows;
the occasion is the funeral of one lovely woman and the marriage
of another. The setting links, rather than contrasts, "a newly
opened grave" to "the open church door" (130). The dead
woman as well as the living bride is headed toward a consummation, and hers is eternal.

The Thanatos-Eros theme often takes the form of a story of
living and dead lovers and, as in *The Bride's Tragedy,* may para-
doxically involve one lover's murder of another as an act of
devotion. For instance, in "The Ghosts' Moonshine" the man
invites his love to "lie under / The tempest bright, my dreaded,
/ In the warm thunder" (95), the latter expression characteristically Beddoesean. Then in the second stanza he identifies the
"pleasant bed" of grasses with what "children call a grave,"
exposed to the cold moonlit night that cannot hurt her, since
she soon will die. In the final stanza the woman quietly says:
"thou hast strangled and slain me, lover, / Thou hast stabbed
me, dear" (96), and it is clear that her murder is a consummation.

Another poem, "Love-in-Idleness," moves through five stanzas of love dialogue marked by an erotic quality unusual in

Beddoes's work to a final stanza in which the female speaker suddenly shifts the poem's tone and direction:

She: Then thou shalt not be my first love, boy,
      nor my second, nor my third;
  If thou'rt the first, I'll laugh at thee and
      pierce thy flesh with thorns;
  If the second, from my chamber pelt with jeering
      laugh and scorns;
  And if thou darest be the third, I'll draw my
      dirk unheard
  And cut thy heart in two,—
  And then die, weeping you.
(124)

The abrupt change here is akin to a similar shift characteristic of Franz Kafka's fiction; sooner or later we are moved from a world of recognizable motivation to a place true only to the writer's idiosyncratic vision. Here the logic of "then" (l. 31) refers us to Beddoes's habitual associations, with no attempt whatsoever at explanation.

A similar associational logic can be found in "The Boding Dreams," where a lover is given a series of prophetic dream warnings that his love will be murdered, this time by another hand. He sleeps on, ignoring the warnings, he himself soothed by death until "the tedious dream is gone" (118). In the last stanza we see the murder take place; the five-line description bears an uncanny likeness to Alain Robbe-Grillet's tableau story "The Secret Room":

A red wound on a snowy breast,
A rude hand stifling the last scream,
  On rosy lips a death-kiss pressed.
Blood on the sheets, blood on the floor,
The murderer stealing through the door.
(118)

Death comments with perfect Beddoesean logic, " 'Now,' said the voice, with comfort deep, / 'She sleeps indeed, and thou may'st sleep?' " (118). Despite the erotic sadism of the above lines, despite the total lack of motive or conventional logic, we have no trouble recognizing Beddoes's peculiar association of love and death.

The "Song of the Stygian Naiades" is a more interesting example of the idiosyncracy of these poems. Here the subject is Prosperine, Pluto, and the latter's amorous impulses:

> PROSERPINE may pull her flowers,
> Wet with dew or wet with tears,
>   Red with anger, pale with fears;
> Is it any fault of ours,
> If Pluto be an amourous king
>   And come home nightly, laden
> Underneath his broad bat-wing
>   With a gentle earthly maiden?
>   (136)

The mermaids of the Styx thus open their song in an amused tone, suggesting that even in Hades husbands may be unfaithful and wives incapable of changing their ways. Browning thought that the poem "wants the 'setting' a little, as one finds it nakedly . . . in print,"[18] but it is not so much Beddoes's failure to elaborate the myth as it is the poem's private associations that account for the way it moves from the clear opening just quoted to the opaque conclusion with its almost Blakean obscurity:

> What hast caught then? What hast caught?
> Nothing but a poet's thought,
>   Which so light did fall and fix
>   'Mongst the flowers and reeds of Styx,
>   Yesterday,
>   Where the Furies made their hay
>   For a bed of tiger cubs,
>   A great fly of Beelzebub's
>   The bee of hearts, which mortals name
>   Cupid, Love, and Fie for shame.
>   (136–37)

Cupid as "a great fly of Beelzebub's" is a striking and resonant image, one that probably compresses much of Beddoes's more serious convictions, and Prosperine's forced and captive marriage to Pluto is never mentioned.

Cupid-as-Death, however, finds less ambiguous expression elsewhere in Beddoes. In one brief fragment the speaker has dreamed that he saw "a thin, pale Cupid, with bare, ragged wings / Like skeltons of leaves in Autumn," and in his wizened little hand he held a weapon more deadly than Love's usual darts. Before the fragment breaks off Cupid promises the speaker that "I shall come, / A death no larger than a sigh to thee, / Upon a sunset hour" (242). And in a short prose piece ("The Tale of the Lover to His Mistress") Beddoes tells the story of a now aged Love who, "after the fall of Jupiter," came by darkness to visit his beloved Psyche. When she attempts to strike a light by which to see the god he prevents her and, after obliquely describing his metamorphosis, he promises her that he is no longer "fleeting, earthly," but "eternal, heavenly Love." Then the moon rises and

Psyche saw beside her a gaunt anatomy, through which the blue o' th' sky shone and the stars twinkled, gold promises beaming through Death, armed with arrows, bearing an hour-glass. He stepped with her to the sea-side, and they sank where Venus rose. (129)

The last sentence is again compressed, but like the lover in "The Ghosts' Moonshine," acquiescence on the lover's part is implied.

This tale is Beddoes's nuclear fable, his ur myth, and the source of much of his symbolism. It explains the concluding lines of "Dedicatory Stanzas," discussed in chapter 4:

> Death's darts are sometimes Love's. So Nature tells,
> When laughing waters close o'er drowning men;
> When in flowers' honied corners poison dwells;
> When Beauty dies; and the unwearied ken,
> Of those who seek a cure for long despair,
> Will learn. Death hath his dimples everywhere;
> Love only on the cheek, which is to me most fair
> (105)

and lies behind "The Two Archers," which restates Beddoes's vision of Thanatos as the true Eros. Undervalued by Beddoes's critics, the poem is one of his finer lyrics. The brief story of fifty-two lines moves relentlessly through a typical Beddoesean arc; opening "at break of bright May morning" the first stanza

paints a vital picture of spring and the lark's joyous ascent,
"winged and all soul into the sky" (131). Stanza 2 describes
a young woman's discovery of two figures in that landscape—
a "wild archer boy" and a "withered bowman." Competing
with each other for her attention, both cry, "come buy our
darts":

> They are with magic laden
> To deify the blood;
> An angel in the bud,
> Half-closed, is a maiden,
> Till opened by such wound she fly
> Winged and all soul into the sky.
>
> (131)

The phallic imagery here is appropriate; in the third stanza she
chooses Love because her "desire / Is for his darts, whose breath
fans higher / The smitten roses like a fire" (132). Love "shot
smiling / His shaft, then flew away," leaving the woman to
lament his going. In the December world of the final stanza
she seeks out Death to "cure a forsaken lady," having come
to realize that his dart "is but for those who'd fly / Winged
and all soul into the sky" (132).

One more late lyric, "The Phantom Wooer," will help to
emphasize both the characteristic content and style of these
poems. The piece opens predictably enough; a dead lover stands
above the bed of a sleeping girl and softly calls her to his own
world. Then in the second and concluding stanza Beddoes
achieves his own peculiar tone:

> Young soul put off your flesh, and come
> With me into the quiet tomb,
>   Our bed is lovely, dark, and sweet;
> The earth will swing us, as she goes,
> Beneath our coverlid of snows,
>   And the warm leaden sheet.
> Dear and dear is their poisoned note,
> The little snakes of silver throat,
> In mossy skulls that nest and lie,
> Ever singing "die, oh! die."
>
> (159)

Here is the very essence of Beddoes's lyrical voice: delicate, intimate, slyly persuasive, sinister, insidious, and above all perversely seductive. There is a hypnotic quality in these lines, especially in the four-line refrain that concludes both stanzas. If his accomplishment in poems like this is not momentous it is all the same impressive, and it is worth noting that a greater poet would one day catch his third line (and something of the entire poem's seductive quality): "The woods are lovely, dark and deep."

As we have seen, behind all these poems, but sometimes, as in "The Phantom Wooer," not overtly discussed, is a profoundly felt but only vaguely formed idealism. Love and Death are identical, and it is through that union that one gains access to the world of permanence. What man calls life is but a "brief parenthesis in chaos" (248) and through death "are all dreams made true, / Ever to the last" (111). In poems such as "Dream-Pedlary," "The Song of the Stygian Naiades," and "The Phantom Wooer" one hears clearly Beddoes's unique voice.

The Lyrical Grotesque

One other strain in Beddoes's nondramatic poetry, a strain limited yet absolutely characteristic, remains to be mentioned. We have seen in *Death's Jest Book* the pained laughter of a humor both astringent and bitter, satiric and self-parodying. He composed an interesting group of poems that, though small, nevertheless vividly reflects this aspect of Beddoes's imagination. Whereas the poems of love and death generally look back to *The Bride's Tragedy,* these works are associated almost entirely with *Death's Jest Book,* and many of them are found as songs in that play. While some few possess, like "Lord Alcohol," an almost relaxed form of humor, typically these works move inevitably beyond what we usually understand by that term. As Ian Jack has remarked, "there is an element of the grotesque in him, something 'Gothic,' unmelodious, unclassical."[19]

Critical attitude toward this element in Beddoes's poetry has changed considerably in recent years. In 1912, for example, Oliver Elton could confidently assert that the "experiments of Beddoes in lyric of the *macabre* kind are made with the utmost relish, but they are apt to overreach themselves and to tire

and disgust the most willing imagination."[20.] Even thirty-six
years ago Samuel Chew could describe the quietly controlled
and innocent drinking song "Lord Alcohol" as a "repulsively
grotesque ditty," [21] a description utterly without justification.
But readers who have come to accept and even relish the black
humor of the late twentieth century have had less trouble appre-
ciating the grotesque vision in Beddoes, recognizing it as a
genuine imaginative response to the absurd.

Something of Beddoes's grotesque humor can be seen in the
previously discussed "Song of the Stygian Naiades." Though
the quality there is subdued, surely his picture of Pluto returning
"nightly, laden / Underneath his broad bat-wing" with yet another mortal woman for his bed suggests something of Beddoes's
usual exaggeration, and still more his description of Cupid as
a "great fly of Beelzebub's, / The bee of hearts" (136, 137).
Another situation from classical mythology produces, in "Silenus
in Proteus," one of Beddoes's rare poems of truly genial humor.
Browning might well have commented that here, too, as in
"Song of the Stygian Naiades," the poem "wants the 'setting'
a little,"[22] but like most writers Beddoes expects us to know
that Silenus was associated with Bacchus and that he was usually
portrayed as a merry, fat, and intoxicated old man astride a
donkey. In Beddoes's poem a very old Silenus looks back with
fondness and nostalgia to a time "when I was with thee and
sat kingly on thee, / My ass of asses" (137). The donkey is
now dead and, because this is a poem by Beddoes, Silenus says
mournfully that he also "shall ride thee soon about the Elysian
meadow, / Almost a skeleton as well as thou" (137). He complains that his "dearest," despite all his "pats and fondlings,"
would simply "die like any other mortal ass":

> Was it for this, oh son of Semele,
> I taught thee then, a little tumbling one,
> To suck the goatskin oftener than the goat?
> (137)

The joke in "Silenus in Proteus" depends in part on the
obvious pun—"I sat upon my ass and laughed at Jove"—but
a genuinely scatological element emerges in an extraordinary
poem, "The New Cecelia." This coarse but comic ballad tells

of the drunken gypsy wife of St. Gingo (who becomes "old
Stingo") and how after his death she denied his sainthood, claiming him no more able to perform miracles "than a clyster-pipe
thunder / Or I sing a psalm with my nether-end" (112). Such
a claim was a grave mistake, for

> As she said it, her breakfast beginning on
> A tankard of home-brewed inviting ale,
> Lo! the part she was sitting and sinning on
> Struck the old hundredth up like a nightingale.
>   (112)

This "Aeolian warbling" became her fate until

>   she did aged die
> Cooing and praising and chirping alert in
> Her petticoat, swung like a curtain
> Let down o'er the tail of a Tragedy.
>   (112)

The poem ends with a tongue-in-cheek warning to ladies who
might undervalue their husbands "lest, ah! well a day! / Such
judgements befall the incredulous / And your latter ends melt
into melody" (112).

It is difficult not to think of Rabelais and Chaucer here, or
any number of earthy poets on the margins of literature. Donner
claims that "there is nothing offensive in the language" of this
poem,[23] and while one may agree, it is yet possible to imagine
the reactions of the squeamish or prudish reader. Beddoes included the poem in a letter to Kelsall, admitting that it was
"a very objectionable piece of foolery, enough to ruin the reputation of anyone, who wishes to introduce his writings into good
society" (663). But he goes on to add that he preferred "The
New Cecelia" and "such like absurdity" to his "Pygmalion,"
the former being "far more poetical" (664). Beddoes is surely
wrong about "Pygmalion," as is Snow, who, agreeing with Beddoes's judgment, calls the poem a "colourless . . . literary
gesture."[24] On the other hand, Beddoes does acknowledge the
vitality of these poems, as well as their honesty of feeling. Taken
generally they may be seen as a gesture toward psychological

and creative integrity; some are obviously self-parodies of his own unusual style and others are intended to mock all that was conventionally pretty. At any rate, "The New Cecelia" is alive and robust, and that fact prompts him to contrast it with the sadly resigned "Pygmalion."

The same vigorous and fertile imagination that produced "The New Cecelia" resulted in another very curious and funny poem, "The Oviparous Tailor." Without any of the implied vulgarity of the previous poem, Beddoes yet suggests one of his peculiar anatomical transformations. The impoverished tailor, only a "small-beer sinner," a "starveling rat," steals the eggs laid by a witch's hen, fellow resident of his tenement. The witch, with a witchlike lack of compassion, curses the wretched tailor and "did all his little luck spill":

> Tho' he swallowed many a muck's pill,
> Yet his mouth grew like a duck's bill,
> Crowed like a hen,—but maler,—
>   Wee, wee tailor.
>
>   (113)

The "but maler" is a touch worthy of Byron's *Don Juan,* and the repetitions, comic rhythms, and rhymes are perfect throughout. Each day laying "above a hundred / Gallinaceous eggs,— but staler," wee, wee tailor continues his helpless metamorphosis until "Fowl-death did prevail," and with that outrageous pun the poem concludes. Despite the tailor's cruel end, the poem exhibits such lightness and verve that here the grotesque appears the result of high rather than low spirits.

But elsewhere the grotesque in these poems may take a grimmer form. Here is a short example, one especially in keeping with *Death's Jest Book:*

> THREAD the nerves through the right holes,
> Get out of my bones, you wormy souls.
> Shut up my stomach, the ribs are full:
> Muscles be steady and ready to pull.
> Heart and artery merrily shake
> And eyelid go up, for we're going to wake.—
> His eye must be brighter—one more rub!
> And pull up the nostrils! his nose was snub.
>
>   (90)

Not surprisingly this piece is called "Resurrection Song" and the concluding couplet snaps the poem shut with a beautiful abruptness that yet allows the reader one brief glance at the naked skull before it is again masked in flesh.

A body travels in the opposite direction in the terrible "Harpagus, hast thou salt enough," a poem of awful revenge, which, while dramatically unintegrated into *Death's Jest Book,* is yet one of the songs most in keeping with the play's mood and tone. When Isbrand realizes his moment of apparent victory over Duke Melveric he sings a ballad that fully represents his moral degeneration. In it he combines the Mycean story of Atreus, who serves his brother Thyestes a dinner made of Thyestes' own children, with the tale of Astyages' similar revenge on Harpagus. The poem opens with a sinister lilt:

> Harpagus, hast thou salt enough,
>   Hast thou broth enough to thy kid?
> And hath the cook put right good stuff
>   Under the pasty lid?
>
> (90)

Harpagus, unaware of the source of his dinner, commends the stew, for "the cook hath mixed the meat and grease / Most tickling to my tooth." Astyages offers him fruit picked "from a tree divine" and when his guest "brushed the leave away" in the basket he

>   saw a face,
> Chopped from the shoulders of some one;
> And who alone could smile in grace
>   So sweet? Why, Harpagus, thy son.
>
> (91)

The next lines are powerful:

> "Alas!" quoth the king, "I've no fork,
>   Alas! I've no spoon of relief,
> Alas! I've no neck of a stork
>   To push down this throttling grief."
>
> (91)

With a mocking apology for his inability to gather up all of the boy's parts, Astyages leaves his victim with the words "good-

night, and digestion be good" (91). The song then tells how
Harpagus, silent in his terrible grief, went on to exact his own
revenge on Astyages. But though this second revenge is Isbrand's real point, the poem's impact is found in the more
graphic first half, the result of Beddoes's peculiar juxtaposition
of tone and detail.

The two songs that best epitomize Beddoes's lyrical grotesque,
however, are "Old Adam, the carrion crow" and "Isbrand's
Song" ("Squats on a toad-stool under a tree"). The first is sung
by Wolfram, by now a ghost but one who nonetheless plays a
fully human role. He has just heard Siegfried (something of a
dandy) sing a poetically conventional song ("My goblet's golden
lips are dry"), and to Isbrand's praise of Siegfried's song he
replies:

> Good melody! If this be a good melody,
> I have at home, fattening in my stye,
> A sow that grunts above the nightingale.
> Why this will serve for those, who feed their veins
> With crust, and cheese of dandelion's milk,
> And the pure Rhine. When I am sick o' mornings,
> With a horn-spoon tinkling my porridge-pot,
> 'Tis a brave ballad: but in Bacchanal night,
> O'er wine, red, black, or purple-bubbling wine,
> That takes a man by the brain and whirls him round,
> By Bacchus' lip! I like a full-voiced fellow,
> A craggy-throated, fat-cheeked trumpeter,
> A barker, a moon-howler, who could sing
> Thus, as I heard the snaky mermaids sing
> In Phlegethon, that hydrophobic river,
> One May-morning in Hell.
>
> (479)

Following the bathetic plunge of these last lines Wolfram sings
his own "Old Adam, the carrion crow," a poem in keeping
with the taste expressed in the above speech.

Wolfram's song is appropriate for Hell on a spring morning,
but there is nothing conventionally devilish about the piece.
In "The New Cecelia" Beddoes had parodied the saints' lives;
here Adam and Eve are re-created as two old carrion crows
of Cairo, not God's splendid new denizens of Eden. Adam sat

> in the shower, and let it flow
> Under his tail and over his crest;
>   And through every feather
>   Leaked the wet weather;
> And the bough swung under his nest;
> For his beak it was heavy with marrow.
>
>   (94)

Though the marrow of kings it is yet like any other human flesh; the condition and fate of the body are everywhere the same. A great queen and a famous beauty can make only a passing nest for birds unimpressed with vanity:

> Ho! Eve, my grey carrion wife,
>   When we have supped on kings' marrow,
> Where shall we drink and make merry our life?
> Our nest it is queen Cleopatra's scull,
>   'Tis cloven and cracked,
>   And battered and hacked,
> But with tears of blue eyes it is full:
> Let us drink then, my raven of Cairo.
>
>   (94)

Donner sees this poem (and the others in this vein) as "capital fun" and offers it as an example of one of Beddoes's random "flashes of brilliance."[25] The poem is indeed brilliant, but its quirky humor springs from what had become by now his fully realized vision of the absurd. Not only Adam and Eve but also Cleopatra (and the unnamed kings) represented a world of illusory significance the poem repudiates. One has only to recall Shakespeare or, closer to home, Leigh Hunt's lovely sonnet "The Nile," with its fine line describing Cleopatra as "the laughing queen that caught the world's great hands," to be able to gauge the reductive force of Beddoes's humor. Its "gallows-music"[26] perfectly captures the general distortion of noble things, and the flash—the poem is only two stanzas long—allows us to see the result by Beddoes's comic light.

"Isbrand's Song" carries this process further. He too rejects the perfunctory and conventional in poetry: "I hate your ballads that are made to come / Round like a squirrel's cage, and round again" (432). Certainly the song he sings is anything but typical of the Romantic lyric. Nowhere is Beddoes's imagination more grotesque, bizarre, idiosyncratic. His friend Procter, never the best judge of poetry, found it "absolutely objectionable," while Beddoes himself considered it "almost necessary to the vitality" of *Death's Jest Book* (645). Swinburne was perhaps the first of many to declare it Beddoes's best poem;[27] certainly it is his most characteristic. The work deserves quoting in full, but these generous excerpts will demonstrate its nature:

> SQUATS on a toad-stool under a tree
>   A bodiless childfull of life in the gloom,
> Crying with frog voice, "What shall I be?
> Poor unborn ghost, for my mother killed me
>   Scarcely alive in her wicked womb.
> What shall I be? shall I creep to the egg
>   That's cracking asunder yonder by Nile,
>   And with eighteen toes
>   And a snuff-taking nose
>   Make an Egyptian crocodile?
>
> . . . .
> "Swine, shall I be you? Thou'rt a dear dog;
> But for a smile and kiss and pout,
> I much prefer *your* black-lipped snout,
>   Little gruntless fairy hog,
>   Godson of the hawthorn hedge.
> For when Ringwood snuffs me out
>   And 'gins my tender paunch to grapple,
>   Sing, ' 'Twixt your ancles visage wedge
>   And roll up like an apple.'
>
> . . . .
> "I'll not be a fool like the nightingale
> Who sits up all midnight without any ale,
>   Making a noise with his nose;
> Nor a camel, although 'tis a beautiful back;
> Nor a duck, notwithstanding the music of quack,
>   And the webby mud-patting toes.
> I'll be a new bird with the head of an ass,
>   Two pigs' feet, two men's feet, and two of a hen,
> Devil-winged, dragon-bellied, grave-jawed, because grass
>   Is a beard that's soon shaved and grows seldom again
>   Before it is summer: so cow all the rest;
>   The new Dodo is finished. O! come to my nest."
>   (89–90)

Jack, almost alone in judging Beddoes negligible as a lyric poet, observes that the song "reminds one of Browning at his most uncompromising," adding that "Beddoes has a liking for rude mouthfuls of consonants and other unacceptable combinations of sounds."[28] The irregularity of his rhymes and rhythms here is obvious, but the only "unacceptable combinations of sounds" are those that will not work. Here the sound pattern is perfectly functional, and fully in keeping with the weird metamorphosis taking place in the poem. This aspect is, in fact, part of the poem's satire on conventional poetry; the nightingale is reduced, after all, to nothing but a bird "making a noise with its nose."

Duke Melveric remarks of one of Isbrand's later songs that "poetry, they say, / Should be the poet's soul; and here, me-thinks / In every word speaks yours" (467). And so it does in this piece. Moreover, the poem reflects Beddoes's vision at its most uncompromising, however comic. The frog-voiced child, an "unborn ghost," has been killed by his own mother while still in the womb. It speculates on various forms of life it might take: crocodile, pig, snake—each with its advantages. It rejects still other forms, including the lovely nightingale, and instead chooses to become a dodo, an absolutely absurd "unity" repre-senting the process of creation turned inside out, rendered ab-surd. Just as Adam and Eve become carrion crows, so the child becomes a strange conglomeration of parts, an inhuman monster. We cannot help laughing at this freak; the laughter, however, is anything but happy. Rather it is the laughter of Beddoes's satirical side, and what he satirizes here is neither social nor moral evil but the very possibility of meaningful life.[29] Like his own Harpagus, Beddoes was forced "to push down this throttling grief," and poems like "Isbrand's Song"—for a little while—helped him do it.

Beyond a certain point we can only guess at the poet's meaning in these poems. They are like splinters of a broken mirror that we imagine once to have reflected some world entire. The best, with one or two exceptions, are brief, illusive, oblique; typically they imply but do not assert, suggest but never insist. Most hint at a spiritual autobiography so private as to be almost en-tirely inaccessible to the reader, and probably even to the con-scious mind of Beddoes himself. And despite or even because of all this, they have long haunted those readers fortunate enough to have discovered them.

Chapter Six

Conclusion

"Once a man is absorbed by an idea there is no doing anything with him," complains one of Chekhov's disillusioned characters.[1] That Beddoes gradually became utterly obsessed with death in all its aspects is unquestionable. He had watched his father dissect small animals in order to instruct his children in the human processes, and then his father died. He had subsequently invested all his familial love in his mother and then, when Beddoes was in the midst of his first success, she too died. From her death we may date his existential as opposed to simply literary preoccupation—in imagery, plot, character, and in cadaver and skeleton. Keats too, in default of imagination's victory over human failure, often flirted with "easeful death." But even while dying he came to see a renewal in the midst of process more satisfactory than any escape afforded by the visionary imagination. Beddoes, however, eight years Keats's junior and destined to live on in a post-Romantic twilight, came to accept the identification of death with imagination itself. As Harold Bloom points out, "for Beddoes the separation between subject and object is bridged not by any imaginative act, as in Blake, Wordsworth, and Shelley, but by dying."[2] Far from becoming a sod to the high requiem, Beddoes pulled the funeral flowers and "through their tendrils" heard "a sweet soft music, like an angel's voice" (234). Henceforth Thanatos was to be his muse.

Romantic artists more nearly faced a common problem than shared common solutions to that problem; the fragmented nature of Romantic experience is even stronger in those late embodiments like Beddoes. But there is nonetheless a strong sense of zeitgeist in his work. He was a poet of great sensuosity like Keats, an explorer of spiritual reality like Shelley, driven toward themes of self-extinction like such German Romantics as Novalis (and modern examples such as Rilke), given to irony like Tieck, Byron, and Heine.

Like Poe, Beddoes concentrated on a no man's land between life and death, a world marked by an "extraordinary co-presence of horror and serenity."³ When other poets, for example Coleridge, had become wearied with the Gothic motif, Beddoes, again like Poe, employed it to convey this peculiar vision. However, his power of conviction is so genuine that the ragged stage properties and hackneyed scenes of a theater essentially the product of popular culture vibrate with a terrible kind of energy, macabre wit, and emotional authority. As with Poe there is a strange but quite genuine humor; unlike that of his American contemporary, it never results from literary games. His grotesque, like that of Baudelaire, is exuberant but very, very serious.

To the association with Poe and Baudelaire we may add two post-Romantic associations, one with Kafka and, beyond him, with Samuel Beckett. As in Kafka, in Beddoes's hands the normal world continually dissolves into a bizarre distortion; as in the work of Beckett his world appears absurd, meaningless. For Beddoes came to see "man's frail and perilous tenure" (491) as essentially absurd in the modern sense of the word. *Death's Jest Book* is not simply the "vivid expression of pathological mental conditions," nor only a "failure of poetic nerve" characteristic of late Romanticism, as Karl Kroeber has suggested,⁴ but clearly more extreme than either. The dejection poems of Coleridge, Wordsworth, and Shelley had demonstrated much earlier the negative potential in the Romantic sensibility. In Beddoes, however, we can recognize a dramatic shift from apocalyptic optimism to apocalyptic despair; in his most important work we witness Romanticism collapsing in on itself, inverting a vision of ever-expanding life into a vision of therapeutic death. He may be, as it has been argued, the last Elizabethan or the obvious link between Shelley and Browning. However, his imaginative power and historical significance can both be traced to his unique dramatization—made possible by his considerable talent and tortured vision—of Romanticism's own self-destructive tendency.

Romantic affirmation was heroic but vulnerable. Among the disturbing signs of its darker side, the litter of unfinished though ambitious works bears particularly painful witness to unsolved problems, growing doubts, the apocalypse denied or distorted.

This element finds its most intense, if narrow, expressions in *Death's Jest Book,* itself in some ways one of Romanticism's great unfinished poems.

The world of mid-nineteenth-century England was not ready for Beddoes's extraordinary mixture of haunted lyric and grotesque humor; the fate of his literary remains in the hands of an admiring but nervous Browning suggests an ironic symbolism—the strange and disturbing is pushed down, submerged, suppressed. Even the experience of the early twentieth century did not liberate an imagination so foreign to the daylight dreams of modern man. But the generation that has come to embrace Kafka as a member of the family may yet, perhaps, come to claim Beddoes as a spiritual ancestor.

Notes and References

Preface

1. Ian Jack, *English Literature 1815–1832* (Oxford, 1963), 144.
2. H. W. Donner, *Thomas Lovell Beddoes, The Making of a Poet* (Oxford, 1935), 381.
3. *The Works of Thomas Lovell Beddoes,* ed. H. W. Donner (Oxford, 1935), 543. All subsequent quotations of Beddoes's writings are from this text unless otherwise indicated. Hereafter cited as *Works* in notes; in text, page numbers given in parentheses.
4. Lytton Strachey, "The Last Elizabethan," in *Books and Characters: French and English* (New York, 1922), 237–65. First published in *New Quarterly* 1 (November 1907):47–72.

Chapter One

1. H. W. Donner's study remains the best source of biographical information.
2. John Heath-Stubbs, *The Darkling Plain* (London: Eyre & Spottiswood, 1950), 42.
3. *Fragmentary Remains, Literary and Scientific of Sir Humphrey Davy* (London: Churchill, 1858), 150.
4. Dr. Beddoes attempted poetry also, and among his publications is the 562-line couplet poem *Alexander's Expedition down the Hydaspes and the Indus to the Indian Ocean* (1792). He was, however, no poet and felt no inner need to express himself that way.
5. Quoted in *Thomas Lovell Beddoes: Plays and Poems,* ed. H. W. Donner (London, 1950), xlix. The colored boots were used as political badges by the *Burschenschaft,* more conventional emblems having been outlawed.
6. Henry James, *Hawthorne* (New York: Harper & Brothers, 1879), 30.
7. Philip Rahv, "An Introduction to Kafka," *Image and Idea* (Norfolk: New Directions Books, 1957), 107.

Chapter Two

1. Quoted by J. B. Beer, *Coleridge the Visionary* (London: Chatto & Windus, 1959), 142.

2. Montague Summers, *The Gothic Quest* (London: The Fortune Press, n.d.), see especially chapter 1, "The Romantic Feeling," 17–56.

3. Northrop Frye, "Towards Defining an Age of Sensibility," *ELH* 23 (June 1956):144–52.

4. See Donner's speculation, *Beddoes*, 60–61.

5. Ibid., 77.

6. *Monthly Review; or Literary Journal* 95 (June 1821):218.

7. Donner, *Beddoes*, 73.

8. See especially Agnes's response: *Works*, 39.

9. Royall H. Snow, *Thomas Lovell Beddoes, Eccentric and Poet* (New York, 1928), 22.

10. Donner, *Beddoes*, 64–65.

11. Snow, *Beddoes*, 22.

12. Donner, *Beddoes*, 75.

13. *Don Juan* 15:2.

14. Ibid., 15:99.

15. Ibid., 15:2.

Chapter Three

1. In 1824 Beddoes had been "turning over old plays in the Brit: Museum" and was contemplating the editing of "another volume of specimens." *Works*, 592.

2. Elder Olson, *Tragedy and the Theory of Drama* (Detroit: Wayne State University Press, 1961), 9.

3. *Letters and Journals*, in *The Works of Lord Byron*, ed. Rowland E. Prothero (London: John Murray, 1898–1904), 5:347. For an interesting observation on "mental theatre" in contrast to the actual stage, see Thomas Hardy's preface to *The Dynasts*. He concludes by noting that "whether mental performance alone may not eventually be the fate of all drama other than that of contemporary or frivolous life, is a . . . question not without interest." *The Dynasts* (London: Macmillan, 1958), 1:x.

4. Kenneth Burke, *Attitudes Toward History* (Los Altos, Calif.: Hermes Publications, 1959), 39.

5. Northrop Frye, *Anatomy of Criticism* (Princeton: Princeton University Press, 1957), 247.

6. Terry Otten, *The Deserted Stage: The Search for Dramatic Form in Nineteenth-Century England* (Athens: Ohio University Press, 1972), 7–8. Otten is of course quoting a famous line in Matthew Arnold's preface to his 1853 *Poems*, an essay designed as his opening attack on Romanticism.

7. Robert Langbaum, *The Poetry of Experience: The Dramatic Monologue in Modern Literary Tradition* (New York: Random House, 1957).

8. Quoted by Claude Colleer Abbott in *The Life and Letters of George Darley, Poet and Critic* (Oxford: Oxford University Press, 1967), 219.

9. *Letters and Journals,* 5:217, 268.

10. Donner points out that these observations were made while Beddoes was at work on "The Second Brother," where he was, indeed, "trying to modernize traditional material," not simply imitate that material. See 167.

11. See note 4, Preface, above.

12. "Thomas Lovell Beddoes: A Critical Study of His Major Work," (Ph.D. diss., Ohio State University, 1968).

13. Allardyce Nicoll, *A History of English Drama 1660–1900* (Cambridge, 1955), 4:201.

14. For the full title and a detailed account see Donner, *Beddoes,* 84–86.

15. Eric Bentley, *The Playwright as Thinker* (New York: Meridian Books, 1957), 163.

16. Northrop Frye, *A Study of English Romanticism* (New York, 1968), 53. Flora was, interestingly enough, Zephyrus's wife.

17. Goode, "Beddoes," 45.

18. Eleanor Wilmer, *Gathering the Winds: Visionary Imagination and Radical Transformation of Self and Society* (Baltimore, 1975), 88, 81.

19. Percy B. Shelley, *Adonais,* ll. 462–63, 458; *The Prelude* (1850), 2, l. 254.

20. This apt expression is found in *Blackwood's Edinburgh Magazine,* December 1823, and is quoted by Snow, *Beddoes,* 45.

21. It was in 1825 that Beddoes made his trenchant observations on dramatic "reanimations."

22. Snow, *Beddoes,* 52.

23. See *Works,* 580, 586, 594, 601.

24. Donner, *Beddoes,* 145.

25. Ibid., 149.

26. Ibid., 152.

27. Frye, *English Romanticism,* 55.

28. Wilmer, *Gathering the Winds,* 74.

29. *Works,* 269, 274, 275, 267.

30. "I feel myself in a measure alone in the world & likely to remain so . . . I fear I am a non-conductor of friendship, a not-very-likeable person." *Works,* 610.

Chapter Four

1. See note 3, chapter 3.

2. Robert Browning, *The Browning Box,* ed. H. W. Donner (London, 1935), 103. Hereafter cited as *Browning Box.*

3. Frye, *English Romanticism,* 63.

4. Verse letter to Thomas Butts, November 22, 1802, l. 88.

5. The toast was made at the painter Benjamin Haydon's "immortal dinner," December 28, 1817. "Cold philosophy": "Lamia," pt. 2, ll. 229–30; 237.

6. Percy B. Shelley, *The Revolt of Islam,* ll. 2255–56.

7. In Jewish mythology the Bone of Luz was that imperishable part of the body time could not destroy. Beddoes says that the bone "is, according to the Rabbins, the only one which withstands dissolution after death, out of which the body will be developed at the resurrection." *Works,* 487.

8. Henry David Thoreau, "The Natural History of Massachusetts" (1842), as quoted by Perry Miller, "Thoreau in the Context of International Romanticism," *New England Quarterly* 24 (1961):148.

9. Richard Selzer, *Mortal Lessons: Notes on the Art of Surgery* (New York: Simon and Schuster, 1976), 19, 16, 39.

10. Karl Kroeber, "Trends in Minor Romantic Narrative Poetry," *Some British Romantics,* ed. James V. Logan et al., (Columbus: Ohio State University Press, 1966), 286.

11. See note 7, chapter 3.

12. Matthew Arnold, preface to *Poems* (1853).

13. Otten, *Deserted Stage,* 9.

14. John Gardner, *On Moral Fiction* (New York: Basic Books, 1978), 14. The italics are Gardner's.

15. Geoffrey Wagner, "Beddoes, Centennial of a Suicide," in *The Golden Horizon* (New York, 1955), 553. Originally printed in *Horizon* 19 (1949):417–35.

16. *Henry Crabbe Robinson on Books and Their Writers,* ed. Edith J. Norley (London: J. M. Dent, 1938), 2:712.

17. *Browning Box,* 103.

18. Harold Bloom, *The Visionary Company* (London, 1961), 430; G. Wilson Knight, *The Golden Labyrinth* (London: Methuen, 1964), 220.

19. C. H. Herford, *The Age of Wordsworth* (London: G. Bell and Sons, 1924), 267.

20. Frye, *English Romanticism,* 57.

21. Heath-Stubbs, *Darkling Plain,* 58.

22. John Dryden, preface to *Absalom and Achitophel* (1681).

23. Ibid.

24. Arnold, "The Scholar Gypsy," ll. 163, 203.
25. Wagner, "Centennial of a Suicide," 552.
26. Ibid., 418.
27. Letter to John Murray, November 3, 1821.
28. Quoted by William R. Mueller and Josephine Jacobsen, "The Absurd Quest," *Kenyon Review* 29 (1967):240.
29. *Browning Box,* 104.
30. Snow, *Beddoes,* 104.
31. Wilmer, *Gathering the Winds,* 75.
32. Act 3, ll. 1543–44.
33. John Agar, "Isbrand and T. L. Beddoes' Aspiring Hero," *Studia Neophilologica* 45 (1973):372. The problem of Isbrand's character has been suggested by Agar, who objects to the general critical enthusiasm for Isbrand's success as an aspiring hero. Agar sees Isbrand as capable only of hatred; he is "the least human of Beddoes' protagonists." Recognizing Isbrand's nihilism and what he calls "his consuming narcissism," Agar reads the play as Beddoes's complete repudiation of the jester: "Nearly every relevant aspect . . . seems to ridicule Isbrand's pretensions." The critic's own disgust with the character appears total, and he especially objects to attempts to link Beddoes with his protagonist. Yet Agar refers to Isbrand's "tragic flaw," alludes to him as a "tragic hero," and generally accepts him as a Romantic character who "seems to transcend the Gothic tragedy of which he is a part." Although his dislike of Isbrand is so comprehensive as to devalue these terms almost totally, Agar's inability to ignore Isbrand's stature—"a Faustian hero of . . . immense power and intellectual complexity"—reminds us of the impossibility of assigning him a simpler role. Clearly Beddoes himself shared Isbrand's nihilism and, if not narcissistic, he was terribly self-isolated and admittedly antisocial. Agar, "Aspiring Hero," 379, 384, 381, 376, 388, 372.
34. *The Poems of Thomas Lovell Beddoes,* ed. Ramsay Colles (London: Routledge & Sons, 1907), preface; Donner, *Beddoes,* 234; Anne Harrex, *"Death's Jest Book* and the German Contribution," *Studia Neophilologica* 39 (1967):33; Knight, *Labyrinth,* 221; Agar, "Aspiring Hero," 384.
35. Frye, *English Romanticism,* 73.
36. Act 2, l. 1036.
37. William Blake, *Jerusalem,* plate 10, l. 20.
38. Wallace Stevens, "Of Modern Poetry," ll. 1–4.
39. William Wordsworth, *The Prelude* (1850), 9, l. 70; 6, ll. 339–41.
40. M. H. Abrams, "English Romanticism: The Spirit of the Age," in *Romanticism Reconsidered,* ed. Northrop Frye (New York: Columbia University Press, 1963), 59.

41. Herbert Lindenberger, *On Wordsworth's Prelude* (Princeton: Princeton University Press, 1963), 120–21.

42. Heath-Stubbs, *Darkling Plain,* 39.

43. Knight, *Golden Labyrinth,* 219.

44. *Thomas Lovell Beddoes, Selected Poems,* ed. Judith Higgens (Manchester, 1976), 14.

45. Frye, *English Romanticism,* 52–3.

46. Important exceptions are Eleanor Wilner (*Gathering the Winds*) and Donald W. Good, "Thomas Lovell Beddoes: A Critical Study of his Major Works." I am indebted to both of these writers in this section.

47. Wilmer, *Gathering the Winds,* 95.

Chapter Five

1. *A History of Nineteenth Century Literature* (New York, 1913), 115.

2. Oliver Elton, *A Survey of English Literature: 1780–1830* (London, 1912), 2:299.

3. Jack, *English Literature,* 143.

4. People in England, except for a few old friends, were equally unaware of Beddoes and would largely remain so, even long after the posthumous publication of *Death's Jest Book* in 1850.

5. Wagner, "Centennial of a Suicide," 549.

6. Alfred Lord Tennyson admired Beddoes, however, and may refer to him in *In Memoriam A.H.H.,* # 34, when he speaks of "fantastic beauty; such as lurks / In some wild poet, when he works / Without a conscience or an aim."

7. The degree to which Beddoes is influenced by Romantic irony remains unclear, despite critical sentiment to the contrary. The mode is illusive and difficult to define, especially in English-speaking writers. Perhaps the most useful speculation can be found in Harrex, *"Death's Jest Book* and the German Contribution." The second section of her study—"Romantic Irony and *Death's Jest Book"*—suggests when, if any, the mode made its greatest impact.

8. *Browning Box,* 139.

9. Kelsall argued that Keats held a "peculiar fascination" for Beddoes and that "Pygmalion" offered the "sole instance of a direct impress from another mind, in the whole compass" of his friend's poetry. The latter claim is too exclusive, but the influence here is obvious. T. F. Kelsall, ed., *The Poems, posthumous and collected, of Thomas Lovell Beddoes* (London, 1851), xxii–xxiii; cf. *Browning Box,* 85–86.

10. Douglas Bush, *Mythology and the Romantic Tradition in English Poetry* (New York, 1963), 194.

11. Donner, *Beddoes,* 174.
12. Snow, *Beddoes,* 148.
13. Donner, *Beddoes,* 169.
14. Ibid., 274.
15. No less demanding a critic than George Saintsbury has declared "Dream-Pedlary" perfect, and Donner has devoted five pages to a detailed analysis of the poem's prosody. *History of English Prosody* (London, 1923), 3:150; Donner, *Beddoes,* 277–81.
16. Snow, *Beddoes,* 145.
17. See especially chapter 3, section entitled "Eros and Thanatos."
18. *Browning Box,* 105.
19. Jack, *English Literature,* 143.
20. Elton, *Survey,* 303.
21. *The Nineteenth Century and After (1789–1939),* vol. 4 of *A Literary History of England,* ed. Albert C. Baugh (New York, 1948), 4:1257.
22. *Browning Box,* 105.
23. Donner, *Beddoes,* 335.
24. Snow, *Beddoes,* 148.
25. Donner, *Beddoes,* 143.
26. Elton, *Survey,* 303.
27. *George Chapman, A Critical Essay* (London: Chatto Windus, 1875), 78.
28. Jack, *English Literature,* 143.
29. Donner, believing the poem reflects Beddoes's spiritual idealism, argues that Isbrand "creates a new habitation for a human soul. The more repulsive the matter, it would seem, the greater the triumph of the mind." Donner, *Beddoes,* 230. Louis O. Coxe adds, "what does this song show us if not the varied aspect of man's nature when he is most self-aware and creative." "Beddoes: The Mask of Parody," *Hudson Review* 6, no. 2 (Summer 1953):260. John Agar is right, however, when he rejects this interpretation; "the name of the animal is itself a comment on it: the child will be a Dodo, an atavism. . . . Surely such a creature is not representative of the 'varied aspect of man's nature when he is most self-aware and creative,' but the opposite." "Aspiring Hero," 382.

Chapter Six

1. The story is "Gooseberries."
2. Bloom, *Visionary Company,* 434.
3. Knight, *Labyrinth,* 219.
4. Kroeber, "Trends," 287.

Selected Bibliography

PRIMARY SOURCES

1. Contemporary editions, arranged chronologically
The Improvisatore, in three Fyttes, with other Poems. Oxford: J. Vincent, 1821.
The Brides' Tragedy. London: F. C. & J. Rivington, 1822.
Death's Jest-Book or The Fool's Tragedy. London: William Pickering, 1850.
The Poems, posthumous and collected, of Thomas Lovell Beddoes. Edited with a Memoir by Thomas Forbes Kelsall. London: William Pickering, 1851.

2. Collected and selected editions
The Letters of Thomas Lovell Beddoes. Edited with notes by Edmund Gosse. London: Mathews & Lane, 1894.
The Poetical Works of Thomas Lovell Beddoes. Edited with a preface and memoir by Edmund Gosse, 2 vols. London: J. M. Dent, 1890.
Selected Poems. Edited with an introduction by Judith Higgens. Manchester: The University Press, 1976.
Thomas Lovell Beddoes: Plays and Poems. Edited with notes and an introduction by H. W. Donner. London: Routledge & Kegan Paul, 1950.
The Works of Thomas Lovell Beddoes. Edited with notes and an introduction by H. W. Donner. London: Oxford University Press, 1935.

SECONDARY SOURCES

1. Bibliography
New Cambridge Bibliography of English Literature, 3:409–11. A short bibliography ending with 1967 entries.

2. Book-length criticism and interpretation
Donner, H. W. *Thomas Lovell Beddoes, The Making of a Poet.* Oxford: Basil Blackwell, 1935. The single most important resource for

Beddoes studies; includes a full biography and comprehensive criticism and interpretation.

Goode, Donald W. "Thomas Lovell Beddoes: A Critical Study of His Major Works." Ph.D. diss., Ohio State University, 1968. Much good analysis of *The Brides' Tragedy* and *Death's Jest Book;* useful source of information on the Renaissance influence on Beddoes.

Snow, Royall H. *Thomas Lovell Beddoes, Eccentric and Poet.* New York: Covici & Friede, 1928. Still useful study, though dated, especially concerning Beddoes's literary sensibility.

3. Parts of books and articles

Agar, John. "Isbrand and T. L. Beddoes' Aspiring Hero." *Studia Neophilologica* 45 (1973):372–91. Interesting for his analysis of Isbrand, hero of *Death's Jest Book,* and hence for the whole play. Sees Isbrand not as aspiring hero but as nihilist.

Bloom, Harold. *The Visionary Company,* 428–34. London: Faber & Faber, 1961. Interesting short analysis of Beddoes's poetic vision.

Bush, Douglas. *Mythology and the Romantic Tradition in English Poetry,* 192–96. New York: Norton, 1963. A valuable discussion of Beddoes's use of Greek mythology; useful also on "Pygmalion."

Chew, Samuel C. *The Nineteenth Century and After (1789–1939).* Vol. 4 of *A Literary History of England.* Edited by Alfred C. Baugh, 1256–58. New York: Appleton Century-Crofts, 1948. Useful short discussion.

Coxe, Louis O. "Beddoes: The Mask of Parody." *Hudson Review* 6, no. 2 (1953):252–65. Valuable assessment of Beddoes's satirical mode.

Donner, H. W., ed. *The Browning Box.* London: Oxford University Press, 1935. An important collection of letters (written by friends and admirers) concerning Beddoes's poetry.

Elton, Oliver. *A Survey of English Literature 1780–1830,* 297–304. London: Edward Arnold, 1912. A sensitive description of Beddoes's poetry.

Frye, Northrop. "Yorick: The Romantic Macabre." In *A Study of English Romanticism,* 51–85. New York: Random House, 1968. The most discerning modern analysis of *Death's Jest Book* and its relationship to Romanticism and Romantic myth.

Harrex, Anne. "*Death's Jest Book* and the German Contribution." *Studia Neophilologica* 39 (1967):15–37; 301–18. A detailed examination of several German influences on Beddoes's work, especially German Romantic Irony.

Heath-Stubbs, John. *The Darkling Plain,* 37–48. London: Eyre &

Spottiswoode, 1950. Strong discussion of Beddoes as a late Romantic.

Jack, Ian. *English Literature 1815–1832,* 138–44. Oxford: Oxford University Press, 1963. Excellent short assessment.

Nicoll, Allardyce. *A History of English Drama 1660–1900,* 4:201–2. Cambridge: Cambridge University Press, 1960. Places Beddoes in the context of contemporary drama.

Saintsbury, George. *A History of Nineteenth Century Literature.* New York: Macmillan, 1913.

————. *A History of English Prosody.* Vol. 3. London: Macmillan, 1923. Brief but perceptive discussions of Beddoes's poetry and prosody by a demanding and acute critic.

Strachey, Lytton. "The Last Elizabethan." In *Books and Characters: French and English,* 237–65. New York: Harcourt, Brace, 1922. First published in *New Quarterly* 1 (1907):47–72. Strachey helped renew interest in Beddoes and gave him his modern title. Good on connections with Renaissance drama but needs qualification as an overall assessment.

Wagner, Geoffrey. "Beddoes, Centennial of a Suicide." In *The Golden Horizon,* 543–61. New York: University Books, 1955. First published in *Horizon* 19 (1949):417–35. Good discussion of Beddoes's modernity, especially of his political and economic views.

Wilmer, Eleanor. *Gathering the Winds. Visionary Imagination and Radical Transformation of Self and Society,* 47–134. Baltimore: Johns Hopkins, 1975. A brilliant if eccentric study of Beddoes's work as a negative example of the Romantic apocalyptic vision.

Index

C